En
fo

We heartily recomm .... concen-
trates on how to pray for inner healing, forgiveness, and deliverance. It is a practical guide, showing a prayer minister how to
administer healing prayer. We hope that many counselors read
Released to Soar and are encouraged to pray for inner healing.
-*Francis MacNutt, Ph.D., Christian Healing Ministries, Inc.*

In the past decade, scientific research has given us a better
understanding not only of the integral functioning of the most
complex organ in our body, the brain, but also the interconnected-
ness of the psychological, spiritual, and physical aspects of our
being. This book brings these components together, documenting
the effect of prayer on two of the most prominent mental health
disorders in our country and the world—depression and anxiety. A
door is now open to gain an understanding of how prayer may initiate a cascade of events that lead to emotional healing. This book,
then, is a must-read for anyone in need of emotional healing.
-*Harold G. Koenig, M.D., Professor of Psychiatry*
& Behavioral Sciences, Associate Professor of
Medicine, Duke University Medical Center

I first encountered Peter and Eleanor Boelens when I was asked
to teach their ministry team how to integrate their faith into their
practice... They listened and became enthusiastic about healing
the many "messed up" people they were encountering. Their
studies and experiences have culminated in this book that accurately, clearly, and persuasively describes the process of Christian
healing and its effectiveness. I am blessed to have played a small
role in their lives to bring about the development of their effective
ministry, and the writing of this book. It is wonderfully well done.
-*William P. Wilson, M.D., Professor Emeritus at Duke*
University Medical Center, Distinguished Professor of
Counseling, Carolina Evangelical Divinity School

Earlier Books about the Previous Ministries of Peter and Eleanor Boelens

Delta Doctor by Peter Boelens, M.D., with Maureen Rank

Delta Doctor traces how God leads Peter and Eleanor Boelens to found and develop a Christian ministry in the two poorest counties of the Mississippi Delta. That ministry, Cary Christian Center, is still active in 2010 and has been highlighted in the *New York Times* and national TV for reducing the infant mortality rate in their service area for the past 15 years.

Where Next, Lord? by Peter Boelens, M.D., with Maureen Rank

As a sequel to *Delta Doctor, Where Next, Lord?* follows Peter and Eleanor as God leads them, in sometimes startling and miraculous fashion, to help Christians in the developing world who share Peter's vision of touching lives through healthcare and the Gospel of Christ. The Luke Society continues this vibrant, global collaboration.

Delta Doctor, Where Next, Lord? and *Released to Soar* can be ordered online at www.thewriteplace.biz/bookplace or with the order form at the end of this book.

RELEASED TO SOAR

A MEDICAL STUDY SHOWS THE POWER OF HEALING PRAYER

Dr. Peter & Eleanor Boelens
with **Maureen Rank**

The life stories in this book are authentic. The names of the individuals, however, have been altered and in some instances life experiences amalgamated to protect their identities.

Style notes: In pronoun references, we have chosen to alternate the male and female pronouns by chapter. The authors prefer using capitalization in pronoun references to God; however, since the Bible translations used have made these references in small letters, they have chosen to abide by that style for ease of reading.

ISBN: 978-0-9825974-4-6

Published and printed in the United States of America by The Write Place. Cover and interior design by Alexis Thomas, The Write Place. For more information, please contact:
The Write Place
599 228th Place
Pella, Iowa 50219
www.thewriteplace.biz

Copies of this book may be ordered
from The Write Place online at
www.thewriteplace.biz/bookplace

The Boelens' online forum for healing prayer can be found at:
www.ShalomPrayerMinistry.com

Dedication

This book is dedicated to the prayer clients who come to us for healing prayer. Their honesty in sharing their innermost hurts and their trust of us as God's facilitators humble and bless us. To the members of our research study group, we give special thanks. Their faithfulness to weekly appointments in the midst of feelings of depression and hopelessness was sometimes a challenge, but they cooperated and persevered.

Contents

Acknowledgments

A person whom I hold in highest esteem is Dr. William Wilson, Professor Emeritus of Psychiatry at Duke University. It was Bill who opened my understanding to this area of the healing of the soul or psyche. He took the time to come to the Mississippi Delta, spending a week sharing his healing insights with staff of the Cary Christian Center and lay home visitors who support them. For this I can not thank him enough.

The individuals who equipped us with a spiritual understanding of how God works his healing through specific prayers are Francis and Judith MacNutt. Their Christian Healing Ministries, Inc., in Jacksonville, Florida, provided structured classes for all desiring to become prayer ministers. Their ministry provided most of the prayers and other forms in this book.

All scientific endeavors involve a critical group of people who add their insights and expertise. I am greatly indebted to Harold Koenig for educating me as to how scientific experiments are designed and then adding his critical insights to the study manuscript. During the four years it took to complete this research project, Roy Reeves, a psychiatrist and accomplished researcher, walked me through the complexities of the scientific protocol and in the process we became kindred spirits. Bill Replogle provided the statistical analysis.

The person who really made this work and the medical study possible, however, is my best friend and soul mate, my wife Eleanor. Eleanor did all the praying with the study clients, and God's healing power flowed through her in a miraculous way.

Introduction

Antidepressant drugs are now a $9-billion-dollar-a-year industry. Depression affects over 121 million people worldwide and is among the leading causes of disability. The World Health Organization estimates that by 2020 depression will be the second-largest health issue in the world.

In the past ten years, my wife Eleanor and I have been practicing a new treatment for Christians who struggle with depression and anxiety. It is known as "healing prayer," but it isn't the same as the prayers we usually employ. It's differently focused prayer—one that is specifically directed toward those with what some call "inner childhood wounding." We view this work as a healing of the soul or psyche. Health of our soul/psyche is crucial to our spiritual, mental and physical well-being. Realizing this, the Apostle Paul prayed that the Holy Spirit would strengthen the inner being of individuals so that Christ could live fully in their hearts unhindered by any brokenness (Ephesians 3:16,17).

The prayer is actually a series of prayer sessions—usually four to six one-hour sessions—done with a prayer minister who has time to listen, love and pray rather than the one-time altar prayer that many churches offer. During prayer sessions, guided prayers are offered for:

- healing from hurtful memories from the client's past and present
- forgiveness for those who have been hurtful
- inner healing for wounds that limit joy and peace, and
- deliverance from any sources of evil that might have hidden God and his gifts of abundant life.

This prayer methodology is based on the understanding that God is not bound by time as we are. He can be as present right now in situations we experienced twenty or thirty years ago as he is in our present situation. Because this is true, it is possible to go back through our memories to situations from the past and invite him to bring his perspective, love and power to those painful situations. Through this process, it is possible to experience an emotional do-over, if you will, and see these painful situations in a different and healing way that gives freedom from the power of wounds to hurt us.

Those who go through this process of inviting Christ into their painful memories say that after healing, they can still remember hurtful events but more incidentally. The severe negative emotion is gone, much as Paul expressed when he said, "Oh, Death, where is thy sting?" Because the pain and other negative emotions have been removed, the memory no longer has the power to cause current pain that can lead to depression, fear or anxiety. Participants report not only a freedom from depression and anxiety (and sometimes even other kinds of healing, such as physical healing), but also almost universally report a heightened intimacy with God and a more immediate experience of his love and care for them.

In one-year follow-up with some of our prayer clients, they said consistently that God met them in a very real way at their point of pain, and changed their experience of the hurtful situation so dramatically that they found freedom from the pain and its after-effects, almost as if it had never happened to them. Many of these participants said they'd prayed about their problems for years—had others pray for them—gone to healing services—and had extensive therapy and medications. But none of these gave the level of forward-movement toward healing as this prayer methodology.

In the pages ahead, we want to share some of our journey and learning with you. You'll understand more about what this kind of prayer is, how it works, and what kinds of effectiveness it has demonstrated. Teaching and case studies *describe* the process of healing through prayer. A medical study *documents* the effectiveness of healing through prayer. Prayer tools *demonstrate* how to practice healing prayer for yourself or others.

You'll also, with their permission, read the actual experience of some of our prayer clients, whose names and life settings have been adjusted to protect their privacy. When you've finished, you may find you want to try the prayers for yourself, or for others you care about who suffer with the aftermath of childhood wounds. In either case, we believe you'll find, as we have, that as we invite him in, God "is able to do immeasurably more than all we ask or imagine, according to his power that is at work within us" (Ephesians 3:20).

RELEASED TO SOAR

A MEDICAL STUDY SHOWS THE POWER OF HEALING PRAYER

Vanished Pain

Sandy came for prayer to heal a sharp pain in her right ear. The pain had no physical cause. But we discovered emotional pain, the residue of a childhood with overly controlling, unpleasable parents. We prayed with her for forgiveness for her resentment toward her parents, and for the breaking of childhood vows she'd made to never be like them.

After our third session we prayed for the pain in her ear. It resolved completely, but reappeared later in the day. This happened again in two more sessions. But as her healing deepened and she experienced more of Christ's love, the ear pain eventually completely resolved. Her propensity to overcontrol her children and to work too hard to please others resolved, as well.

CHAPTER ONE

Wounds Are Real, but God Can Heal

"He forgives all my sins and heals all my diseases;
He redeems my life from the pit and crowns me
with love and compassion."

PSALM 103:3-4

As a physician, I've had one focus for the past five decades: using my medical training to help people—both in the U.S. and in more than a dozen other countries—to find relief from their illnesses, pains and wounds. I've treated maladies as simple as scabies and as complex as paragonamiasis, all to one end: that those who are suffering come out of their misery to life and health.

In the last ten years, I've come to understand that hundreds of thousands, perhaps millions of people, are hemorrhaging from wounds that aren't visible in the way a flesh wound is visible. Yet these wounds are every bit as debilitating—even life threatening—as any case of systemic infection I've ever treated. I've realized that thousands of patients I've treated during my career have been suffering from these unacknowledged wounds, but I left them undiagnosed and untreated. My oversight didn't come from lack of compassion for my patients; I simply didn't understand what could be done with the root causes of some of the maladies I was observing. Even if I had understood causes, I wouldn't have known how to treat them.

The wounds I'm describing aren't physical; they are emotional injuries I now call *wounds of the soul or psyche*. They came from moments when the psyches of my patients were attacked, whether in childhood or as adults, and their souls were left raw and bleeding, in a way that was as palpable as if an attacker had grabbed a knife and stabbed them through the heart. These wounds now show themselves as depression, anxiety, relationship schisms, physical illnesses, and even suicidal intentions.

But along with discovering the existence and implications of these inner wounds, my wife Eleanor and I have also found a way to help, with a treatment intervention that a recently-published medical study has found to be effective in 85% of patients who received it (see **Medical Study Appendix C**). The treatment is . . . healing prayer.

Prayer? Certainly a great support alongside medical treatments, but prayer *as* the treatment? Before your skeptic-meter kicks into overdrive, as mine once would have, join me as we better understand the problem. Then let me share a little of our journey toward prayer as a treatment.

Inner Wounding: First, the Bad News

Inner wounding is happening, and these wounds are taking a toll. Over half of children in our society are raised in homes where parental addictions, abuse or divorce are realities. Some estimates say 50% of these children will be severely wounded and will grow up with emotional and relational problems. Very often, these childhood wounds show themselves in depression and anxiety—rampant issues in our world. At any given time, 10% of the United States population experiences depression, and 18% an anxiety disorder.[1] From a global perspective, depression

[1]Kessler RC, McGonagle KA, et al., Lifetime and twelve-month prevalence of DSM-III-R psychiatric disorders in the United States: Results from the National Comorbidity Study. *Archives of General Psychiatry* 1994; 51:8-19.

is common; about 121 million people worldwide are affected. These are serious problems, indeed.

Now the Good News

The good news is this: God has provided a way out of this dilemma. Jesus died not only for our sins but also for our wounds. *The Message* puts it this way, "It was our pains he carried—our disfigurements, all the things wrong with us" (I Peter 2:24). Because he carried our pains and wounds, he is able to heal us.

His healing is wholistic: spirit, soul and body. I believe that's his intention for us, as expressed by the Apostle Paul when he said, "May your whole spirit, soul and body be kept blameless at the coming of our Lord Jesus Christ" (I Thessalonians 5:23). God intended to make his home in all three "components" of our being: our spirits—the part of us that connects directly to God's Spirit—and our souls, or *psyches*, in which our personality, thoughts, emotions, memories, imagination and will reside. He wills that our bodies be healed, as well, because his wholeness was intended to touch all our being. The way we've uncovered to administer his healing is through a process of *innercession*, a particular kind of prayer.

Innercession isn't like the prayers for others you may be familiar with. Prayers of intercession ask God to do something *to* others' suffering. In *innercession*, God enters *into* the moment that generated the suffering, removing debilitating emotions attached to painful memories, and recreating these memories as places of grace. We call it "removing the scarring of the soul."

We believe in *innercession* because we've seen proof, both experiential and empirical. Over the past ten years we've worked with many clients who report healing prayer resulted in dramatic changes for the better in their lives. Also, we've conducted a randomized, controlled study with 63 prayer clients that demonstrated marked improvement (see **Medical Study Appendix C**).

There is even more good news. Utilizing this prayer methodology doesn't require a medical degree or training in either psychotherapy or theology. Administering it to others can be done by a compassionate, teachable lay person with faith in a God who works through prayer and some understanding of the tools of healing prayer.

A Picture of Innercession at Work

Does all I've described sound too good to be true? It may, depending on the mental pictures the words "healing prayer" bring to your mind. These may vary greatly, depending on your theological orientation and which television preachers you've been exposed to. May I clarify for you what I mean when I talk about healing prayer? In agreement with the maxim, "a picture is worth a thousand words," let me tell the story of our healing experience with a prayer client I'll call Nicole.

Nicole was 31 when we met her, but we soon learned she'd lived several lifetimes of pain in those 31 years. Abandoned to foster care by her parents, Nicole's life was a blurry series of abuses. There was the foster mother who whipped her with a pizza paddle for not making the bed correctly. Another time she grabbed Nicole and another foster girl in her care by their hair and slammed their heads together. A second foster home that seemed at first to offer security in the arms of a kindly mother figure turned into a nightmare as Nicole experienced sexual abuse from her foster father and two neighborhood teens. A third foster mother fulfilled Nicole's dreams by deciding to adopt her, but before the process could be completed, the woman was diagnosed with breast cancer and had to abandon the adoption.

In her final foster family before she ran for her freedom, her adoptive mother regularly subjected her to beatings that threatened her life. (In this family, her 13-year-old adopted brother confessed he had asked his parents to adopt Nicole because he knew she was old enough to beat but too small to fight back. "I was hoping they'd pick on you and leave me alone...so now it's your turn.")

In one particularly gruesome experience, the woman beat Nicole to the floor with a broom handle, and slammed it hard enough to break it. She lunged toward the cowering girl to stab her with the jagged point of the broom handle. At the last moment, Nicole grabbed the woman's calves and pulled herself through her legs, confusing her attacker long enough to get away. Soon after Nicole ran away from home, and at 15 ran away a third time, and for good. Besides the incredible damage to her body and soul, her spirit had been attacked, as well.

Later, with the help of a kindly pastor, she would hear the story of God's love, and decide that her own attempts at finding love—during the years on her own in the arms of men who only took advantage of her—hadn't succeeded. She gave her life to Christ, later married Howard, and through his mother's influence, both began to grow in faith. But in the midst of this new life, all was not well.

Though Nicole read the Bible and was active in service, she still felt a deep sense of emptiness. "Going forward" at her church for deliverance or healing would alleviate the pain for a little while, but then it would come back. And then there were the "episodes" where a reminder of the family and kindness she had missed growing up would prove to be so painful Nicole would literally slide down into non-stop sobbing for a day or two before she could pull herself together enough to go on with life. She even entertained thoughts of suicide. "I don't understand it," she told us. "How can I belong to God, love Jesus, and still feel so miserable I sometimes want to die?"

As Nicole told us her story in our first healing prayer session, Eleanor looked at her kindly. "Maybe you need to let the Lord heal the hurts from your past," she said. With this invitation to hope, we began a five-month journey with Nicole in which she experienced healing prayers.

During our time together, we joined Nicole in a generational healing prayer, in which she reviewed wounds from her family's abandonment and invited Christ to fill the void she felt with his love and care. We went together in prayer into the abuse and shame that had been inflicted on her, and saw Christ meet her there, too, showing her in very personal ways that she had never been alone. She worked through forgiveness for all who had left her or hurt her—and came to a point of such release that she could even pray blessings for them, instead of the curses that had been part of her desire for them before.

As healing became real to Nicole, we—and others—could see the changes. She told us of feelings of hope and joy and love that were replacing the emptiness and darkness that had filled her. She began to even look different, as baggy clothes were replaced by fitted, attractive ones. ("I was afraid that unless I looked awful, men might hit on me and cause me pain. I used to pray that God would scar my face so no one would want me for what I looked like. But after God's healing, I know I no longer need to hide the person God made and loves. I'm safe now in him.") She even came to the point of finding both her biological father and mother, with mixed responses from them.

For Nicole the experiences only brought a fresh sense of her strength in Christ, and a renewed confidence that her past was no longer binding her. She could forgive and see the people in her past for who they were and are, and then leave them, wishing for them the life in Christ she had found.

We'll talk more later in the book about lessons we learned as we walked with Nicole through each of the stages of her healing. But at this point, I must back up and offer a confession. When Nicole first told us her story, I thought, "This woman could be in psychotherapy for the rest of her life and still not function normally." Any sense of personal adequacy I may have entertained flew out the window. Eleanor was thinking the same thing. She told me, "Humanly speaking, there is nothing we can do to help Nicole." But we saw God, through these times of prayer, bring Nicole into healing in a way that was nothing short of supernatural. Her new life helped convince Eleanor and me that something beyond us was happening in these simple prayer sessions; indeed, that healing prayer "works."

My Personal Journey to Innercession

You've just read about a different way of praying for healing and about how convinced we are this prayer methodology can help millions to find freedom from the wounds of childhood. However, I have to admit that if you had come to me several years ago with the information I just shared, I might have raised an eyebrow, tightened my hold on my copy of the *Physicians' Desk Reference*, and asked, with a touch of incredulity, "Are you suggesting prayer instead of Prozac?" Since I'm now a passionate healing prayer advocate, you may be curious about how a Midwestern medical doctor made such a leap in thinking about treating depression and anxiety.

I have to start with a foundational point in my spiritual journey—an experience that happened in the middle of a most unlikely location for holy encounter: Cook County Hospital, in Chicago. I was in the middle of my internship, intellectually and professionally firing on all cylinders. However, spiritually, I was empty, and beginning to feel desperate about feeling empty. Not that I wasn't a person of faith; I had been raised in the church and trusted Christ as my Savior as a child. Also, it wasn't that I lacked commitment. I'd actually chosen medicine as a profession from a sense of wanting to serve others, perhaps as a missionary doctor.

The outside stuff looked pretty good, but inside I knew the heart connection to God I heard others describe wasn't there for me, and I'd been on a personal search for the past five years to try to find that real, tangible, transformational God-touch that others told me was possible. Also, if I was going to be a missionary, wasn't there a source of spiritual power I needed to find? Though, as I said, I'd been searching for five years, on this night, after suturing together a man rife with knife wounds on his face and body, I came back to my room at the hospital dorm, and spiritually "hit the wall." I'd sat down on the bed, with plans to reach for my Bible and the commentary on Romans I had open there, but instead I slumped. It was as if a depression engulfed me. Five years of searching, reading, asking, listening, to no avail. What more could I do to connect to the God I sought? I heaved a sigh. "God," I said, shaking my head, "I am giving up... not on you, but on ever finding you in any personal way."

The next happening was something I'd never experienced before, or have ever experienced since, to the same dramatic degree. Suddenly it was as if the wall, ceiling and floor of that room were made of diamonds and a hundred searchlights were turned on them. I had never seen such brilliance, and I knew it was God showing his presence to me through this visual manifestation. Interestingly, this light didn't evoke fear; rather, I felt engulfed in warmth and love. Though I'm not a person given to emotional extremes, I began to cry, no, sob, and to sing songs of joy. I felt like running from the room, grabbing the first person I saw, and telling them what a wonderful God I had!

What a moment! The light faded eventually, but the clear sense that God had come to me personally was implanted forever. My life began to change dramatically. A spirit of fear that had always bound me disappeared; I took on life with new boldness. Instead of Bible reading feeling like a duty, I consumed God's Word like a starving man would attack a buffet. The trust in him I'd longed for was simply there. I had absolute confidence that he would make right choices for my life, and I couldn't wait to follow him into whatever he planned.

His plans were quickly revealed, through Matthew 9:35. It says, "Jesus went through all the towns and villages, teaching in their synagogues, preaching the good news of the kingdom and healing every disease and sickness. When he saw the crowds he had compassion on them, because they were harassed and helpless, like sheep without a shepherd." This is what I was to do with medicine: go into communities teaching people the causes of disease and how to stay healthy, preaching the good news of salvation and healing all their diseases, using my training as a physician.

The years of ministry ahead were wonderful—the Lord gave ideas and opportunities, and blessed our work in his name, first in South Korea, then in the Mississippi Delta, then throughout the world through an organization called the Luke Society, now active in more than 30 countries. However, during these years of ministry, one quandary always gnawed at me. In these community health ministries I was helping people physically, and even bringing some of them into a first encounter with Christ. However, I was never able to bring them beyond their acceptance of him into that experience of spiritual fullness that had come to me while at Cook County Hospital so many years ago.

When we retired from the Luke Society, my wife Eleanor and I decided to seek fresh ways to make a deeper spiritual impact on the lives of people. We started a small house church and people came to Jesus, but again, they never moved on to a positive, radiant, abundant life. It was frustrating for them, but more so for us. I felt like I was flying an airplane at 1,000 feet, and getting tossed up and down by the thermals, but all the time longing to cruise at 40,000 feet where the ride was smooth.

About this time the same God who met me at Cook County Hospital was once again at work. It began with a provocative conversation with Dr. Bill Wilson at a Christian Medical and Dental Association conference. Bill was a psychiatrist, formerly the chairman of the Department of Psychiatry at Duke University, but instead of discussing medical interventions, he told me about bringing the healing presence of Jesus into the lives of severely traumatized individuals—through prayer. Not long after, I heard Dr. Dale Matthews, an internist at George Washington University, describing a study that he did with forty rheumatoid arthritics. Individuals were assessed for joint swelling, joint mobility and blood chemistries, and then *prayed for* for three days. A year later, follow ups showed that prayer for healing affected a change as significant as introducing an effective new drug regime.

These two conversations stuck to me like glue. It was clear from both physicians that emotional and physical healing took place with their patients. However, I was more intrigued by the spiritual outcomes of approaching these presenting problems with prayer. They reported finding the *spiritual intimacy* with Christ I had been longing to help others discover. These physicians started in a place where I was familiar—people in pain—and had found a way to move them, not just out of the pain, but into closeness to Christ. I needed to know more. Dr. Matthews pointed me to an organization called Christian Healing Ministries in Jacksonville, Florida, who had formed the prayer teams in his study. Eleanor and I arranged a meeting with the organization's founders, Francis and Judith MacNutt. Their spiritual maturity and many years of experience convinced us, and we trained with them as healing prayer ministers. (The work we do today had its foundation in the ministry of the MacNutts, and we'll always be grateful for their teaching and equipping.)

Back in our home in Vicksburg, Mississippi, we thought and prayed about how to begin using the prayer tools we had learned. An opportunity came quickly, though at first I didn't realize that it actually was an opportunity.

After church one Sunday I was chatting with an elderly lady, and in the spirit of social small talk, I asked, "How are you?" "I'm hurting in my shoulder," she complained. Years of medical training kicked in; I knew she was suffering from tenosynovitis or bursitis. I assured her that in time she would be well with some anti-inflammatories and range of motion exercises.

However, that afternoon, the thought came strongly to me that I should ask this lady if I could *pray* for her healing.

"Lord, I really don't want to do that," I resisted. "What if it makes me look foolish?" The thought came back, "You don't have to do it, Peter, but if you don't, you will be missing a blessing." Well, fear of looking foolish is one thing; missing a blessing is quite another. So, that evening when I saw her at church I asked if she would like Eleanor and me to pray with her. To my surprise, she agreed, and we arranged to meet her later in her home.

So, here we were, sitting in a circle, physician and his wife with their newly acquired prayer training, unsure how to begin. I sat there for a moment, then called on an old wisdom: when you don't know what to do, do what you know. I was new to healing prayer, but ah, I knew diagnostic intake interviews, so off we went. I asked her where it hurt and had her go through the range of motion, watching for the areas of pain that she was experiencing. We then prayed for her healing, laying our hands on her hurting shoulder.

After our first prayer, I remembered from our training that unforgiveness could be one of the greatest blocks to healing, so I asked her if she had any unforgiveness in her heart toward anybody. She considered the question, and I told her she could pray silently in confession to the Lord. When she finished, we prayed for her a second time; afterwards I asked how she felt. "Very peaceful," she reported. I asked her to raise her arm. When she did she said, "Oh my. I can extend it much further without any pain." Better, but not yet healed. We prayed a third time; after this she had nearly complete range of motion without any pain.

God was telling us that he was in the healing business, and he wanted us to join him in this work in a way we hadn't before. These prayers would become the vehicle that would enable us to bring people into the intimate relationship with Jesus that I have experienced after God transformed my life. Ten years and scores of clients later, that's exactly what's happened. We're neither trained psychotherapists nor ordained ministers, yet God has worked through the application of simple prayers and people who are willing to let him lead them into healing. We believe this same healing is available for all who suffer the effects of childhood emotional damage. And, we believe the capacity to minister through these prayers to suffering ones is available for all who are willing to trust and learn.

The Theology and Science of the Approach

The theology, if you will, that drives the power of healing prayer is found in Ephesians 3:16-20. It says this:

I pray that out of his glorious riches he may strengthen you with power through his spirit in your inner being, so that Christ may dwell in your hearts through faith. And I pray that you, being rooted and established in love, may have power, together with all the saints, to grasp how wide and long and high and deep is the love of Christ, and to know this love that surpasses knowledge—that you may be filled to the measure of all the fullness of God. Now to him who is able to do immeasurably more than all we ask or imagine, according to his power at work within us, to him be glory."

For a ministry of healing prayer, this Scripture provides anchor beliefs to guide us.

- God wants us to live with power and strength in our inner being, not brokenness.
- Christ "at home" in us means he occupies every room, even closets that are currently filled with junk from childhood wounds and related sinful lifestyles.
- He intends that we be established in love—rooted deeply in love in ways that won't change or move. This rootedness is intended for body, soul and spirit.
- Outcome of healing is being filled with the fullness of God, not just an absence of pain.

- When we come to him, we can expect he is able to respond and *will* respond, and do so in ways that exceed what we could ask or even think.

This book was created with three intentions in mind: to give hope to the wounded that healing is possible; to teach the use of simple and effective tools to people-helpers to connect the wounded to God's healing touch; and to point them to a sovereign God who is intimately concerned with us as individuals, who cares deeply for us and our problems, and who wants to have a loving, mutual relationship with each of us.

As for the science of healing prayer, we'll shift now in the chapter ahead to look at current research in the science of how the brain works, and celebrate together how God's gift of *innercession* is a wonderful application of the way God created us to function, and to change.

Fewer Battles

During a follow-up conversation, Emily spoke with a big smile that radiated warmth. "I have peace now," she explained. "Before prayer I battled constantly. Now I'm able to deal with myself and others peacefully. My husband says I'm a different person, more loveable, less fault-finding. We can talk better together.

"My thinking about who I am has also drastically changed. I now see myself as a special person in God's eyes. You know," she said thoughtfully, "I really like myself."

CHAPTER TWO

Change Your Mind, Change Your Life through Prayer

*"Let God transform you into a new person by
changing the way you think."*

ROMANS 12:2 (NLT)

Though prayer and God's healing are always mysterious, new discoveries in brain science support the wisdom of using a methodology like healing prayer to break free from long-standing emotional wounds. By changing your mind, you can change your brain. When your brain changes, your life changes. A brain change that leads to life change is what God does through healing prayer.

Mind over Matter Is More than a Slogan

It's important to know something fairly basic about your brain. Though we use the words "mind" and "brain" interchangeably much of the time, your mind and your brain are *not* the same thing.

Actually, many scientists, psychologists and psychotherapists thought they *were* the same thing. As far back as the early 1600s, French philosopher Rene Descartes touted the concepts

that have influenced materialism, a dominant scientific phi-
losophy of our time. Materialism means we can only trust to be
real what we can experience with our senses. A brain is a clear
physical entity that can be observed and measured. Therefore
it is "real." But a mind? How do you see a mind? How do you
measure it? How do you hold onto it? Without clear answers to
questions like these, materialists would say the mind is simply
another name for the function of the brain. And if the genes and
neurotransmitters we were born with, encoded in our DNA, don't
work well, and we wind up depressed or anxious, we're trapped.
We're doomed to live like slaves to our less-than-perfect genes
and deficient neurotransmitters.

However, our minds are much more than three pounds
of grey matter. Indeed, recent science tells us that our minds
can control, and can actually change, our brains. For instance,
even though in near-death experiences a person's brain stops
functioning, there have been people who could very accurately
describe what took place, even what was said, during the process
of resuscitating them. Without a physically functioning brain,
how might this be possible? Or what about the report from a
patient who was blind from birth reporting being able to see and
report with accuracy what was happening during resuscitation
from a near-death experience?[1] If our thoughts, perceptions,
feelings all exist only in a physical brain and that brain is dead,
there'd be no way for these experiences to happen.

Nobel Prize-winning neuroscientist John Eccles in his
seminal work studying nerve synapses came to a view that dif-
fered from the materialists. His research led him to believe that
the brain and mind are two different entities.[2] The brain is physical; the mind—including our perceptions, thoughts, emotions,
intentions, memories, dreams and creative imaginations—is
beyond the physical, or the material. We can't see the mind,

---

[1] Kenneth Ring and Sharon Cooper, *Near Death and Out of Body Experiences in
the Blind* (Palo Alto, CA: William James Center, 1999).
[2] John Eccles and Daniel N. Robinson, *The Wonder of Being Human: Our Brain
and Our Mind* (New York; Free Press, 1984), p. 36.

can't touch it, but it not only exists, it can act on the physical brain in ways that change the brain, and as a result, create changes in us. (We'll come back to this later.)

One reason I've had little trouble believing that the mind and brain are not only two entities, but can act definitely on each other, started with experiences in medical school. I was working as a nurse assistant on the 40-bed medical ward of Cook County Hospital in Chicago. Some patients had trouble sleeping because of the noise and commotion on such a large ward, and each night they would plead with me for help. What was a young medical student to do? I wasn't authorized to prescribe sleeping medications, but I wanted to help. So, with more moxie than prudence, perhaps, I finally announced to them with all the authoritative presence I could muster that there was a new and very powerful medication that would cause sleep, but which could not be given on a regular basis because of its potency. I then went on to draw 0.25 ml of saline into a syringe and inject it. The next day on medication rounds, I inquired about their sleep. Each who received the "powerful medication" told me, "It was the best sleep I ever had."

I soon learned that my experience wasn't unique. For example, when antidepressants first hit the marketplace, Janis Schonfeld enrolled in a drug study at UCLA.[3] Schonfeld, a 46-year-old interior designer and single mother, was contemplating suicide and was desperate for help. The medication she was given caused nausea but it changed her life. Her depression was so much improved by the study's end she was able to once again function normally. What was this wonder drug? As it turned out, Schonfeld had actually been assigned to the control group and received nothing more than a sugar pill. However, the hope generated by taking this pill, and her belief in its effectiveness brought about the change. A different way of thinking actually changed her brain.

---

[3]Gary Greenberg, "Is It Prozac or Placebo?" *Mother Jones*, November/December 2003.

The same was true for Sylvester Colligan of Beaumont, Texas, who could barely walk before a 1994 knee surgery he received as part of a research project. After the surgery, he was mobile and pain-free for six years. However, at the end of six years, he was informed that he was actually part of the control group, so no actual surgery was performed; a surgeon simply made an incision in his knee and closed the incision with no change to his knee.[4] Yet because his mind accepted the surgical intervention as real and effective, his brain—and then his body—responded in kind.

A study with similar results was conducted in 2004, evaluating the effect of embryonic stem-cell implants to treat Parkinson's disease.[5] Those who thought they had received stem-cell implants were doing better after one year even though they had received sham surgery.

Indeed, the placebo effect is considered so prevalent and powerful that drugs cannot be licensed by the FDA unless their effect is greater than a placebo.[6]

Childhood Experiences Impact Brains, So Healing Needs to Impact Brains

It doesn't take a highly trained scientist to observe that growing up in an environment of constant trauma makes a difference in who we become, how we view life and the choices we make as adults. Even actor Leonardo DiCaprio has been quoted as saying, "Ninety percent of the people I meet are dealing with issues they can't overcome because of bad parenting. That's the truth. That stuff stays with you forever. You want to say, 'Get over yourself! Come on! Time to grow up!' Some people are able to do that, but a

[4]Barbara Lantin, "Healing Can Be All in the Mind," *Daily Telegraph*, October 25, 2002.
[5]C. McRae et al., "Effects of Perceived Treatment on Quality of Life and Medical Outcomes in a Double-Blind Placebo Surgery Trial," *Archives of General Psychiatry* 2004; 61:412-420.
[6]Placebos usually help people in a control group about 35 to 45 percent. For a drug to be statistically significant it must be at least 5 percent better than a placebo.

lot of us remain victims of it."[7] The new science of epigenetics is offering better explanations for why "Get over yourself" doesn't offer hope for those still carrying scars from childhood. Epigenetics helps us see that those scars are embedded in our brains.

Dr. Moshe Szyf of McGill University in Montreal studied two groups of rat pups, looking for a better understanding of the effects of childhood experiences on how our brains develop. In one group of rat pups, the mothers spent a lot of time licking and grooming their pups—a rat-version of "caring parenting." In the other group, the pups were not licked or groomed; in other words, neglected. The better-cared-for pups grew up to be better adjusted and less fearful than those that were neglected, and also nurtured their own pups in the same manner they had been cared for.[8]

This observation wasn't earth-shaking. What was new came from brain studies of these rat pups. Dr. Szyf found that in the hippocampus, that part of the brain that deals with stress and memory, the better-adjusted rats had a more active version of the gene that encodes a certain protein that made the animal respond to stress in an appropriate, productive way. As a result, they demonstrated fewer behaviors deemed anxious and fearful. In contrast, the brains of the neglected pups released chemicals that *inhibited* this gene from expressing itself in a normal way, so anxious and fearful behaviors were exhibited. More distressing, this tendency to a deficit in this gene expression was passed on to the next generation of pups. The rat-parenting skill, whether good or bad, became self-perpetuating.

However, we're talking about rats here. Does this study point to any conclusions for human parenting? Other research suggests it does. For example, data tells us about 20% of people who commit suicide were abused in childhood. Studying the brains of suicide victims with a history of abuse, and comparing them with brains of those who died of accidents, a definite difference emerged. Those who had been abused showed a much

---

[7]Leonardo DiCaprio, *Parade Magazine*, October 1, 2008.
[8]Ian CG Weaver, Moshe Szyf et al., "Epigenetic Programming by Maternal Behavior," *Nature Neuroscience* 2004; 7, 8: 847-854.

higher level of a chemical that changes normal gene activity in a way that negatively impacts their brain's mood center. In other words, they were chemically less well-equipped to handle stress in a healthy and appropriate way.

Here's the point: you do not need to remain captive to the negative aftermath of childhood wounds. A brain transplant can be yours. A well-known evangelist tried to console a woman struggling with the pain of childhood abuse, "There will be healing in heaven." Of course there *will* be healing in heaven, but Eleanor and I have shared experiences with over 150 clients in the past 10 years in which healing happened in the here and now.

If healing depends on changing our brains, how do we begin?

1. Willful mental activity is the most effective agent in changing brain function.

You can direct how your brain will change by how you focus your thoughts. There are 100 billion neurons in the brain that have 100 trillion connections with other neurons. The firing of neurons produces a gigantic number of possibilities as to the path that will be taken. If you focus on just one possibility, all other possibilities collapse and you've physically moved your brain toward realizing that one possibility on which you've focused.

For example, in Obsessive Compulsive Disorder the neurons in the brain are constantly firing, "telling" a sufferer to wash his hands or check the locks on all the house doors over and over and over. When an OCD sufferer is taught that neurons firing in his brain are driving these thoughts, he can choose to stop them and turn his thoughts to other more productive things. Consequently, he becomes able to control his disease.

If you are interested in living with greater peace and joy, you might choose to focus on the instruction from I Peter 5:7NLT, "Give all your worries and cares to God, for he cares about what happens to you." When you do this, all other thoughts connected to worries and anxieties collapse. If you hold on to this thought, it works like exercise does to strengthen your physical muscles; your brain increases its capacity to believe the truth.

2. Treatment also needs to include attention to emotions, not just thoughts.

Childhood trauma can stay with us into adulthood, and even pass on a propensity for lessened coping skills to our children. We now know, also, that experiences from childhood don't just reside in the cold facts of what happened like textbooks we once read. Memories have the capacity to retain an "emotional sound track" that plays powerfully whenever the story of childhood trauma is recalled. We aren't held captive simply by the facts of the abuse; it's the *feelings* accompanying the abusive experiences that are sometimes more powerful than the facts in driving behavior. Eric Kandel, a Nobel Prize-winning neuro-researcher, has shown that remembering a feeling results in the *release of hormones* that affect both our mental decision making and our body.

As it turns out, this "emotional" view has more power in how we make decisions than does our cognition. Marketers figured this out, after discovering that extensive questioning of buyers about which products they preferred brought in a boatload of useless data. Deciding objectively between products, consumers said they'd choose this one or that. However, when they actually went to purchase, their money didn't follow their cognition!

Something else was at play. So marketers began using MRIs (magnetic resonance imaging) to determine consumers' preferences. People lying inside MRI scanners were shown various products and asked to choose between them. Then, what they said about the products was compared to their emotional responses to the products, as evident in their brain scans. As it turned out, when the area of the brain that indicates pleasure lighted up, the product was more likely to sell successfully—whether they *said* they would buy it or not. Subconscious emotional decisions, not head-generated decisions, ruled the pocketbook.

So, to experience healing from childhood trauma, it isn't enough to simply decide to think differently about it. Both your conscious, rational brain, and your subconscious emotional mind need to be touched in order for new and healthier decision-making to result.

Science tells us that childhood wounding and the negative emotions they evoke are connected through something called *cathexsis*. Cathexsis is a strong, psychic energy that binds the memories and negative emotions together. Getting healed, getting freed, requires breaking this binding between memories and emotions—that's exactly what is accomplished in healing prayer through forgiveness and inner healing.

3. Treatment will be even more effective if it introduces positive emotions that increase a sense of well-being.

Dr. Kandel also discovered an area of the brain in mice, the striatum, whose function is to reinforce a capacity for good feelings. When this area of the brain is stimulated, generating an experience of positive feelings, a secondary outcome is a reduction of fear and an increase in well-being. With this observation, Dr. Kandel offered that perhaps "therapies that enhance the neural circuitry for safety and well-being might well provide a more effective approach to treating anxiety disorders."[9]

This is perhaps the place where we have seen healing prayer generate the biggest—and most surprising—changes. Over and over, now in scores of cases, we've seen clients not just exhibit a sense of relief from no longer being pounded by hurts and wounds, but these same clients actually erupt with joy and buoyancy. Their report of the prayer experience uses words like, "feeling so loved," and "wrapped in Jesus' arms," and "protected, cared for, free." In these prayers of *innerces-*

[9]Kandel ER, *In Search of Memory: The Emergence of a New Science of the Mind*, New York: W. W. Norton Company, 2006, p. 342.

sion, the Lord doesn't simply remove the negative, he fills with the positive power, grace and warmth of his Holy Spirit.

Validating the Science of Healing Prayer: a Four-Year Medical Study

I didn't decide to do a medical study of the effectiveness of our prayer methods because I thought God needed to prove to me that his intervention met my scientific standards. But after Eleanor and I had been conducting the healing prayer ministry for five years, we had seen dozens of people released and spiritually renewed, and in relatively short periods of time, compared with the time investment we had come to expect from traditional psychotherapy. In our enthusiasm about these healings, I began to share our results with colleagues, just as I would have if I had found a new and very effective way to treat heart disease or diabetes. However, just as I would have been many years before, they were skeptical.

As a medical doctor, I must confess that many of us are rightly skeptical when it comes to what sounds like "magic cures." We spent a lot of years learning about the systems and intricacies of the human body, and help others by knowing a lot about what keeps the body from working well, and what can make it work better. Most of us have heard through the years from patients or advertisers about some new herb or pill or light therapy that provides an instant cure for a chronic disease. That's why medical journals continue to be standard-setters for us. We know their published studies have met rigorous tests for their use of proven protocols and replicable methodology. If the intervention "worked" for the authors of the study, we have some measure of confidence it might work the same way for us, if we were to try it.

So, if the medical community had confidence in healing methods that had been investigated by medical journals, why not conduct a study of our healing prayer clients, using a reliable scientific methodology, to demonstrate the effectiveness of this approach to healing depression and anxiety? As a physician I was confident what we were seeing in our clients was genuine and sustained change. Also, I was sure God wasn't threatened by his methods being subjected to scientific scrutiny. After all, wasn't it Jesus who told a leper he had healed to "go, and show yourself to the priest as a testimony?" (Mark 1:44). In first century Judea, priestly pronouncement of cleanness was necessary for lepers to re-enter society. These priests served as the medical journals of their day, and Jesus was confident his results could stand up to their scrutiny. I decided to follow suit.

First, I looked to see what medical science knew already about healing prayer so a study wouldn't duplicate already existing work. I found numerous works showing the effect of religious practices on depression and anxiety; in most of these cases they were positive. However, I couldn't document any clinical trials of person-to-person prayer in the field of mental illness, particularly for anxiety and depression. Most previous studies of prayer examined the effect of prayer over distance (instead of face-to-face) and focused on physical health outcomes, rather than mental health, as we had been doing. A study of these healing prayers would be unique, and would add to, rather than simply repeat, already existing work.

The first step in creating the study was to gather a panel of respected authorities in the field to help with its design and supervision. I served as the study's author, drawing from both my medical experience as a pediatrician, and as Assistant Clinical Professor of Pediatrics at the University of Mississippi. Others co-authoring were:

- Roy R. Reeves, DO, PhD, Associate Chief of Staff for Mental Health at the Jackson, Mississippi, VA Medical Center, and Professor of Psychiatry and Neurology at the University of Mississippi
- William H. Replogle, PhD, Professor and Director of Research, Department of Family Medicine, University of Mississippi Medical Center

- Harold G. Koenig, MD, Professor of Psychiatry and Behavioral Sciences, as well as Associate Professor of Medicine, Duke University Medical Center and Geriatric Research, Education and Clinical Center, VA Medical Center, Durham, North Carolina. Dr. Koenig also co-authored the book *New Light on Depression: Help, Hope and Answers for the Depressed and Those Who Love Them.*

With the collaboration of this stellar team of medical researchers and clinicians, we were ready to design a randomized study of the effect of prayer on depression and anxiety. We also decided to evaluate the presence or absence of positive emotions in the study subjects, and to measure their salivary cortisol levels—a "medical" test, if you will, of how effectively stress levels were being lowered by prayer.

Here's how the study was set up. After being randomly assigned to either a prayer intervention or control group, subjects completed a battery of assessments focused on their mental and spiritual health. (For those of you who follow research more closely, the assessments included the Hamilton Rating Scales for Depression and Anxiety, Life Orientation Test, and the Daily Spiritual Experiences Scale). Participants also underwent measurement of salivary cortisol levels.

All participants in this trial met diagnostic criterion for depression, and most also had anxiety or symptoms of anxiety. They represented a mix of Protestant, Pentecostal, Catholic and non-denominational beliefs. The group—like our population of prayer clients—consisted of mostly women (60) and just a handful of males (3). Most participants showed a commitment to spirituality, demonstrated by praying daily to God for healing. They were 18 or older, and free of any chronic disease or evidence of cognitive impairment. Also, if they had received steroidal medication in the preceding two months, or if they had been treated with psychotherapy during the preceding year, they were eliminated from the pool of potential participants. Those taking antidepressants or antianxiety medications had to commit that the dosages of these medications wouldn't change for the duration of the study. Clearly, we were out to eliminate as much as possible anything but prayer as a factor in changes they reported.

As you may recall from high school science classes, a randomized, controlled study means participants are divided into two groups; half receive treatment and half don't; then their outcomes are compared. Also, the "randomized" part means the division can't be made with an intent to bias the outcome of the study so we're evaluating as reliably as possible what difference prayer made. There was no statistical difference between the control and intervention groups in terms of sex, race, age in years, or prevalence of depression or anxiety. After assigning participants to groups, those selected for prayer received six weekly one-hour prayer sessions, while those in the control group received none.

During the prayer sessions, no psychotherapy was offered. After the prayer sessions were completed, we provided no prayer intervention during the following month or any other counseling, psychotherapy, or medication changes. Rating scales and cortisol levels were administered to both groups after completion of the prayer sessions, and again a month later.

Results of the Study

This is what we wrote: *"At the completion of our trial, **participants receiving the prayer interventions showed significant improvement of depression and anxiety, as well as increases of daily spiritual experience and optimism, compared to controls.** Participants in the control group did not show significant changes during the study.*

"Forgiveness prayers and prayers asking God to come into traumatic memories served to separate the traumatic memories from their associated negative emotions. The memory exists but as an isolated incident without emotional connections. The memory stands as a fact of life without emotional significance.

"Our rational decision-making is processed by our emotions. When negative emotions are unlinked from hurtful memories, participants are freed from their compromised emotional appraisal system. Without [this] limitation, unhealthy thought patterns can be changed with much less effort and greater success."

Science Can Point the Ways to Healing; God Can Actually *Heal*

We celebrate what we've learned from brain science about driving change. It only means that as God leads his people to seek his healing touch through a methodology like healing prayer, he's showing us how to synch beautifully with the ways he created our bodies to function. Also, we celebrate that even though his work needs no validation from science, his touch is so real, so powerful, that it is easy to validate, using scientific methods.

However, much more significant than these is the greatest cause for celebration: the radiance on the faces of clients who have actually been delivered by Jesus through healing prayer. Women and men bound for decades by childhood wounds with no hope are finding freedom, joy and intimacy with the living Christ. Praise God!

You can participate in this ministry of healing. In the chapters ahead, we will share the simple tools we were taught and have used for over ten years, and give you clear direction on how to use them to minister Christ's grace and redemption. You won't need ministerial training to do this work, just a commitment to Jesus Christ and a willingness to listen to and learn from his Spirit as he directs you in sharing his love and power with those in pain. We can tell you from personal experience he will provide in abundance!

And of course, we must add an important dictum of medicine: *do no harm.* To avoid harming clients who might be borderline psychotic, we encourage you to align yourself with physicians, pastors or mental health professionals who can provide guidance.

Moment in a Garden

Ralph owned a successful business, had a lovely wife and two children, and had trusted Christ. His outward life looked enviable; his inner life was falling apart. Memories of sexual abuse by his fourth grade teacher, and again in his teen years by a family friend, consumed him. Even prescription sleeping pills gave no respite from the constant torment.

He was able to forgive his attackers, but still needed healing for his emotions. When we prayed for inner healing, Ralph found himself in a beautiful garden with green grass, fragrant flowers and songbirds. Then Jesus appeared, holding out his arms. "You are my child; I love you very much, and I will care for you," he said to Ralph.

This was Ralph's healing moment. The pain of the memories disappeared, and peace and rest returned, along with a strong sense of Jesus' love and acceptance.

CHAPTER THREE

Preparing the Way for Healing Prayer

*"Get the road ready for the people. Build the
highway. Get at it! Clear the debris...Tell the
daughter of Zion, 'Look! Your Savior comes, ready
to do what he said he'd do, prepared to complete
what he promised.'"*

ISAIAH 62:10 (THE MESSAGE)

When Jesus healed people, he didn't sit in his house in Nazareth or Capernaum and order up a global "fog" of healing that
would spread over all the land and change everyone who suffered
and wanted deliverance. As the Omnipotent God, he certainly could
have brought healing in this way. After all, as he himself declared,
"I am the Lord, the God of all mankind. Is anything too hard for
me?" (Jeremiah 32:27). But the revelation of Jesus as we find it in
the Gospels shows God choosing a very different methodology.
He healed all who asked; this much is clear. But the deliverance of
this healing came one at a time, face-to-face.

Healing in the New Testament happens in stories: stories
involving real people with names, children, circumstances.
One was a woman with a bleeding problem that had gone on
for twelve years, and who had exhausted all her finances trying
the currently available medical treatments—all to no avail. One
was a Roman centurion whose favorite servant had fallen ill.

One was a father with a demon-possessed son who suffered sei-
zures. One was Peter's mother-in-law, whom Jesus lifted from
her bed of illness, and who went straightaway to start preparing
dinner for her guests.

Ministering the Touch of Jesus

Healing in the New Testament is a clearly personal encounter
with Jesus. And after his ascension back into heaven, subse-
quent stories of divine healing all followed the same process,
the process Jesus himself had modeled for his followers. Those
with faith to minister Christ's healing had one-on-one encounters with those in need of Jesus' healing touch, and together
they shared the experience of Christ's power and deliverance
in the life of one in need. I think about Peter responding to the
needs of the crippled beggar at Jerusalem's temple, telling him,
"Silver or gold I do not have, but what I have I give you. In the
name of Jesus Christ of Nazareth, walk!" (Acts 3:6). The Scriptures tell us Peter took him by the right hand and helped him
up. Christ's healing power met them, and the man then leapt to
his feet, walking and jumping and praising God.

　　This story, and others like it, create for me a picture of
how God transmits his healing. One in need of healing, like the
crippled beggar, encounters a child of God with a heart to help
others, like Peter; and in response to a request for help, believers in Christ are able to lead those who suffer to an experience
of Jesus' healing in their lives. I can tell you from experience,
when these encounters take place, it isn't just the sufferer who
is changed. Being a part of a process in which Jesus transforms
a broken one will transform you, too. Healing prayer isn't
just something Eleanor and I do to bless others. We are richly
blessed, as well, as our faith in Christ and sense of partnership
with him has grown, and is growing, as we are part of bringing
his healing to people looking for a way out of their troubles and
a way to God. It necessitates our being "prayed and praised up"

since unforgiveness or neglecting our personal time with God may well prohibit him from using us fully.

How does healing work? Sometimes it is instantaneous; other times it is a process. Consider the woman Jesus healed in Mark 5. She appeared to be instantly healed the moment when she touched his clothes, but this wasn't the end of her healing. Jesus understood the frustration and anger she may have carried after giving all her money to physicians who had provided no relief. Perhaps this is why he said, "Go in peace and be freed from your suffering." He had healed her, but to move forward in life, her soul had to be freed from the suffering of resentment and bitterness toward the physicians who had left her destitute. We find the same to be true in our healing prayer sessions. God's healing for individual hurts is instantaneous, but finding freedom from the suffering generated by a lifetime of hurts can take many sessions.

We begin a healing prayer relationship with three relationship-building steps:

1. Hearing the client's story
2. Bringing them to some understanding of who they are in God's eyes, and
3. Praying to clear away any interference from the Evil One.

Our intention is to end one relationship and begin another. The relationship we're beginning is the start of a trusting partnership between the clients and the prayer minister. As a prayer minister, you are not the source of healing; God is. You are not above or better than or "more together" than the client; neither are you the one with all the answers or the possessor of the Magic Secret they've been seeking. You are simply Christ's servant, willing to join with the client through the next few weeks (or sometimes months) in seeking the experience of Christ's healing touch. You are committed to being a trustworthy, loving, respectful and faithful companion on the journey, but you are not the source of healing; Jesus is. In the pages ahead, we'll talk about practical tools we use to help clients share their stories, and begin the planning of steps for their journey.

However, in the session we also intend to end a relationship. We want to end any connections the clients may, knowingly or unknowingly, have had in the past with evil forces and the occult. The prophet Isaiah spoke of building a highway for God, and clearing away debris. We believe as prayer ministers we are helping to make a highway, a path, if you will, that the client can walk toward Christ. But that path may have debris in the way that makes walking it impossible. Some of that debris can come from Christ's eternal enemy, Satan himself, and his work accomplished through occultish influences or things as simple as hurts experienced in early childhood. The debris of occult practices must be cleared before clients can begin the journey toward a deeper experience of Christ's love, care and freedom.

Confronting Evil

This idea of an Evil One trying to obstruct the path may be new to you. Perhaps your exposure to Christian doctrine didn't include teaching on the reality of Satan and his warfare against God and the people of God. Or at the other end of the continuum, those who've talked to you about spiritual warfare may have presented what sounded like a drama-filled, somewhat frightening, the Devil-is-behind-every-rock viewpoint that may have left you wanting to avoid the whole topic.

I had a moment like this myself a number of years ago when my wife and I were visiting a Luke Society ministry in Zambia. Our driver spoke often of Satan and his influence in daily life. One day he was driving us along a Zambian highway and was simply, by anyone's estimation, driving both too fast, and too close to the median. And sure enough, Wham! He got close enough to an oncoming van that the van tore the driver's side mirror off our vehicle when we passed it. Our driver pulled over to the side of the road, and prayed loudly, "Lord, thank you for delivering us from the devil!" I had to speak. "Joshua," I said, shaking my head. "The devil didn't put us at risk; your driving did. You were just going too fast and not being attentive enough to where we were on the road." Now, our friendship was such that I could speak openly and he could respond with grace. But I tell this story to make clear that I don't believe that the devil is to be blamed for all our troubles, nor does God intend that we live fearful, jumpy lives, always worried about where and how the next blow from the devil will land.

However, I do believe it is clear from Jesus' teaching that just as he came to the world to bring light and life and salvation, both Christ and his people have an enemy with the opposite intention. Consider the following Scriptures:

- Jesus refers to the devil as "the prince of this world" (John 14:30).
- The devil in an instant showed Jesus all the Kingdoms of this world and said, "I will give you all of their authority and splendor, for it has been given to me and I can give it to anyone I want to" (Luke 4:6).
- John makes the statement "that the whole world is under the control of the evil one" (I John 5:19).
- Realizing the extent of the power and activity of Satan, Paul says, "our struggle is not against flesh and blood ... but against spiritual forces in the heavenly realms." He then goes into the protective armor we need and how it is to be utilized (Ephesians 6:10-18).
- The good news is that the "Son of God appeared to destroy the devil's work" (I John 3:8). This is why as we move in the authority and power of Jesus the gates of hell itself can not stop our progress as we reclaim lives from the grip of Satan in the name of Jesus (Colossians 2:15, Matthew 16:18).

In the Lord's prayer, we are instructed by the Savior to pray for "deliverance from the evil one" (Matthew 6:13). And in his great High Priestly prayer for us recorded in John 17, "My prayer is that you ... protect them from the evil one" (John 17:15). I believe Christ both instructed us and modeled for us, making the issue of Satan and his work a matter of prayer because he was fully aware of not just the reality but also the intentions of this enemy. In John 10:10 Jesus warns us of the evil one, one Christ refers to as 'the thief,' and his desires for us. "The thief comes only to steal and kill and destroy." Then he goes on to assure us of his intention toward us. "I have come that they may have life and have it to the full."

The contrast couldn't be more dramatic. From one, destruction and death; from the other, life and fullness. Fortunately, in this war between good and evil, we are very clear, not about who will win, but about who has already won. In his death and resurrection, Jesus Christ defeated all forces of evil. That's why "the one who is in you is greater than the one who is in the world" (I John 4:4).

(We'll talk in later chapters more about instances of the evil one's work in attempting to disrupt the effects of healing prayer, and more importantly, how to stop his interference. But for now, it is enough to know that in this work you have both a friend and an enemy, and that the enemy is not only defeated for eternity, but can be defeated today, in each client's life, by your leadership in resisting him.)[1]

As you begin to serve as a prayer minister, you are coming to clients from the side of life and fullness. The one you represent desires to "proclaim freedom for the prisoners and recovery of sight for the blind, to release the oppressed, to proclaim the year of the Lord's favor" (Luke 4:18-19). Your task is simply to bring prayer clients to Jesus, who will provide the healing. With that end in mind, let's look together at practical ways to open your relationship, and remove any satanic impediments, so healing prayer can go forward with wisdom and compassion and without impediments.

---

[1] We've found books by Doris M. Wagner, *How to Cast Out Demons* (Renew Books, a Division of Gospel Light, Ventura, CA) and Francis MacNutt, *Deliverance From Evil Spirits: A Practical Manual* are particularly helpful.

Beginning the Session: Establishing Christ's Presence

No time of healing prayer ever involves just two people, or three, if you're working with a partner. An additional, though unseen, Presence is always present as we come in his name to accomplish his purposes. It's this Presence, Jesus Christ himself, who does the healing as we remove barriers to his work in our lives and choose to receive his love and goodness.

We work to make sure our clients become aware that Christ is with us, and with his power and help we're going to seek—and find—healing. Looking through the eyes of Jesus, we see a hurting person filled with anxiety and fear. To ease his anxiety we explain what healing prayer is. We tell the person we are not only human beings living in a physical world, but also spiritual beings living in a spiritual world. In this spiritual world forces of God and of evil both reside. Since God is more powerful than Satan and his demons, we can begin with a prayer binding the demonic spirits in the name of Jesus to prevent their interference with the healing God wants to give. We ask, "Does this make sense to you?" (No one has ever doubted this. Their wounding allows them to intuitively understand forces of evil are at work in their lives.) In an attempt to relieve anxiety, we explain that they can relax. They are here to receive—to take in the love and healing of Jesus.

We open the session by asking God to draw from them the busyness of the day and any anxieties and fears they may have, and replace these with his love and peace. We invite the Holy Spirit to come into the session and fill all of us with his truth, love and guidance. Any spirits not of Jesus are commanded to leave in the name of Jesus and go to Jesus for his disposition.

Hearing the Client's Story

When Jesus encountered two blind men on the road from Jericho, he asked them, "What do you want me to do for you?"

(Matthew 20:32). After you've invited Christ to be with you, the client needs to establish his agenda for healing prayer. Jesus dealt respectfully with people, and does with us today. When we begin a healing prayer relationship with clients by listening carefully and compassionately to their story, we show this same respect. When this is done in an attentive, non-judgmental way that demonstrates the unconditional love of Jesus, it can be healing in itself.

For us, a significant part of the answer to "what do you want Jesus to do for you?" comes as we review the **intake form** completed by each client. (A reproducible copy of this form is included in the appendix.) When I first began learning about healing prayer, this step in the process felt the most reasonable, and the most familiar because of my years as a physician. As you know, it's impossible to see caregivers from chiropractors to massage therapists without completing some kind of history. We don't do this to intrude; we do it because we need a way to establish context for our conversation with you.

When patients came to my office with chest pain, most believed that they were having a heart attack. To immediately embrace their conclusion without a history or a physical examination is something no competent physician would do. A good friend of mine began experiencing severe chest pain. He drove to the emergency room where he was told the source of his pain was not a heart attack, but stress. I had several patients who thought they were having angina only to discover on physical exam that they had an inflammation of the junction of the bone and cartilage in their rib cage. When I pressed these affected areas, lo and behold, they experienced the same pain they thought to be angina. A good intake can help make a solid diagnosis.

Clients come to prayer sessions seeking relief from pressing personal problems. For them the intake form is a way to begin telling their life stories. We explain that addressing their immediate problem will require that we go back to their earliest memories of hurt. The reason? One wound has been layered over another in a way that accentuates their present problems. To heal the present, God needs to heal the past. The intake form becomes a vehicle to recall potentially painful details that need God's healing touch. As they enumerate these pains—things like a parent's alcohol addiction or the client having been the result of an unwanted pregnancy—they begin to gain insights about how these events could have significance for their lives in the present.

We usually take notes while we listen in order to remember key points in their history. It's critical to remember we're not listening so we can tell them what we think their root problems are, or to suggest anything remotely close to a solution. We're not doing psychotherapy; we're establishing a relationship so we can come together to Christ for healing.

When we listen, we may ask clarifying questions to help our understanding of where they've been, but it isn't critical we know every detail of their pain or wounding. We are interested in providing a safe, respectful, *confidential* place in which they can speak in trust, because it is in acknowledging the truth of the past, and then letting that truth be cleansed and healed by Christ's truth that we find freedom.

We have clients who require more than one session to tell their story, such as Nicole, whose story we'll explore later in more detail. Because her parents' abandoning her as a child resulted in multiple and extensive episodes of abuse, and because the recounting of all this was very painful, the hearing simply took longer. However, even if we will need to revisit some of the story in a second session, if a great deal of emotional pain has been experienced during this session, we like to let this time come to a close with some focus on hope.

One client reinforced the need for this approach when she told us about a previous experience she'd had in counseling. She recalled, "I would go back into the hurtful memories with my therapist and share some of my deepest feelings. At the end of the session, I hardly had the strength to move, and yet I had to get up, return home and begin preparing supper for the family. It was hurtful and frustrating; there was no healing." So, at the end of this period of disclosure, we pray a prayer that enables them to center on God's love for them. This may also be a time to explore their salvation if they indicated uncertainty about this.

Where do you go next in prayer after the intake history has been obtained? Though leading others through healing prayer isn't as cut-and-dried as following a recipe, we can tell you from personal experience that the Holy Spirit will be a faithful guide, just as he promised.

We often begin with exploring any previous encounters with the occult because we live in a spirit world that we cannot see with our physical eyes. There are demonic forces attempting to influence everyone who seeks to receive—or minister—healing. Some of our clients have let demons in through occult practices such as séances, consulting with fortune tellers, satanic worship and a host of other practices. (A sheet of specific **Occult Practices** is included in the appendix). Before Jesus begins his healing, these doors to the occult need to be closed by the client.[2]

Prayer Focus: Renouncing Occultish Influences

We need to help facilitate the renouncing of evil influences, clearing away this debris so the client can move forward in sessions ahead toward healing.

We use the following explanation to help the client understand why, at this point, we're paying attention to the presence

---

[2]Some may have received the demonic through generational blood lines. We give them the **Preparation of Family Tree** form you'll find in the appendix to take home and fill out, telling them to check each item that is true of themselves or anyone in their blood line. They might find it interesting to fill in the included **Family Tree Diagram**, as well. After these forms are returned to us we lead them through the **Prayer for Healing of Generational Predispositions** found in the appendix. We also teach them to begin to counter their own troublesome predispositions by finding Scripture that speaks God's healing to each one.

of evil in their experience, and helping them to renounce these influences. We tell them:

1. We live in this physical world as a body and as a spirit in the spiritual world.
2. The spirit world is composed of God, his angels and Satan and his demons.
3. The devil comes to steal, kill and destroy while God comes to give life to the full (John. 10:10).
4. The power of God flowing through the prayers we will pray together are able to reclaim the areas Satan has destroyed in their lives.
5. With this understanding it's possible to see why it would be important for us to bind Satan in the name of Jesus. We don't want him to interfere with healing. We want to remove his presence and influence and replace it with God's power and influence.

With these truths clearly in mind, we then explain that we need to know where there might have been openings in their lives through which Satan may have entered. If there are open doors, they need to be closed. And so, we ask them to take a few minutes to complete the 48 questions that are part of the **Occult Practices** sheet.

If we find—and we very often do—that the client has had some connection, whether intentional or not, to the occult, we invite them to pray a prayer from their heart, asking for God's forgiveness for any connections to evil, and renouncing the powers of darkness going forward. The prayer is this:

CLIENT: Lord, I confess that I have...(name occultish acts). I see these now as sins, and I ask your forgiveness by the blood of your cross.

PRAYER MINISTER: In the name of Jesus, these are forgiven as if they had never been.

CLIENT: Thank you, Lord, for this forgiveness. I renounce you, Satan, and every hold you have had on me. I command you in Jesus' name to depart from me and trouble me no more.

PRAYER MINISTER: I take the Sword of the Spirit, the Word of God, and cut you free from every bondage to the occult world. I close the door between you and that world and seal it with the blood of Jesus and bar it with his cross. Walk carefully in your healing, asking the Lord's protection, staying close to his Word and his people.

Concluding the Session

After this prayer, we encourage the client that we've made a good beginning toward healing. With a clear focus on Jesus and his promise to help and heal, we've come to better understand some of the places where healing is needed, and we've cleared the way for Jesus to come by renouncing evil. We remind them that the Scripture tells us to "Submit yourselves to God. Resist the devil, and he will flee from you" (James 4:7). They've just done both during this time of prayer.[3]

Now, with a clear focus on God and his Word, our next session together will create a new understanding of why they were created, and the value they have to God and to others. They'll come to see themselves more clearly from God's view, and begin to access his strength to seek healing and release.

We leave the client with **Scripture verses, such as hope and trust**, with instructions to pray them every day, letting them sink into both mind and soul. We often suggest, "Meditate on these verses and see which ones God emphasizes to you." They have believed Satan's lies about them; now it's time to soak in God's truth.

Preparing for the Next Session:

As you can see, this first session truly does begin the work of "building a highway for our God." You've begun to build a rela-

---

[3]This may be a good time to introduce the **Submission Prayer,** if their spirit seems ready. If not, continue to pray for them and wait for God to work.

tionship of caring and trust with the client that represents God's care for them, and you've together bound evil influences that could have kept the prayer experience from being fruitful.

We find that some clients report that the simple act of telling their story to safe, respectful listeners in itself leads to a measure of healing. You may find this to be your experience, as well. But whether the session seems fruitful or not, we know Jesus cares about these clients, and wills their wholeness. To that end, we pray, and ask others to pray, during the week that they will experience the Lord's love, comfort and hope, and be strengthened to receive healing.[4]

---

[4] If you haven't asked others to join you in this ministry by praying for your clients, this is the time to find such **intercessory prayer** partners. You'll learn, as we have, that this support makes all the difference in seeing brokenness replaced with wholeness, and sorrow turning to joy. We meet with a small group weekly in Vicksburg and send the list to about 25 others. To protect confidentiality, clients' names are changed, or only first names used as we share general requests for prayer. Joy Lamb's wonderful book, *Sword of the Spirit, the Word of God: A Handbook for Praying God's Word* (Lamb's Books, Inc.) gives many Scriptures in categories that fit clients, and has been a useful guide for intercessory prayer groups. Praying Scripture is powerful.

A Dove on Her Shoulder

Mary came with a hurtful story of abandonment by her parents, a series of foster homes, and sexual abuse.

During prayer, she found herself taken to heaven. Jesus was standing in front of an altar. He turned her around and dusted all the dirt off her back; she felt completely cleansed. Then he told her it was time to return to earth. When she objected, he said, "I have something you can take with you," and placed a white dove on her shoulder.

"Do you want to pray for additional healing?" I asked her. "Oh, no," she replied. "Jesus dusted me off and all that hurt is gone."

CHAPTER FOUR

Seeing Life through New Eyes

"You created my inmost being; you knit me together in my mother's womb. I praise you because I am fearfully and wonderfully made. Your eyes saw my unformed body. All the days ordained for me were written in your book before one of them came to be."

PSALM 139:13-14, 16

I remember the first time my computer locked up. The screen was frozen; hitting the keyboard or moving the mouse had no effect. Obviously a problem capable of causing this level of disruption would require a major repair intervention! Where should I look for a technician to attempt it? How long would the computer be out of commission?

Imagine my surprise when a call to the tech center generated this advice: *Why don't you shut it down and reboot?* Could a fix be this simple? As you probably have guessed, the repair was, indeed, that simple. Reboot. Hit the "reset" button. Stop and just start over.

Going Back to Go Forward

If only life were this simple. For many of our prayer clients, this would be a dream come true. One client in particular, a woman I'll call Ruth, comes to mind. Ruth, a petite, attractive young mother of three, came to her first prayer session weighed down with wounds from the past that felt to her like they'd be impossible to escape. As a child she had been molested by her father, ignored by her mother, and ridiculed by her classmates. As she told us about her past, there wasn't a bright spot in her recollection other than the fantasies she created to escape her torment. Her current life was wrapped in just as much darkness, as she lived with emotional, physical and sexual abuse from her husband. How does someone possibly begin to heal from a lifetime of such savage wounds? How wonderful it would be if we could offer her a way to start over, to begin life again.

Here's the good news: it *is* possible to begin again, to hit the "restart" button in your life. We offer just this hope to prayer clients, through a particular prayer experience called the "**Conception to Birth Prayer**." For Ruth, this prayer allowed her to go back to the moment of her conception, and learn from God himself who she was created by him to be. Through the cleansing and re-teaching about her worth this encounter with God provided, Ruth was able to go forward into other healing prayer experiences with new faith and strength.

Does this sound like a far-too-mysterious hocus-pocus? It isn't. Think for a moment about the nature of our God, and what time means to him. For us, time is sequential; there's our past, our present, our future. But God is eternal; he is equally and currently present at every moment in time. Therefore even though a moment in our lives is past to us, it can be completely present to him. That's why he can say, "Before I formed you in the womb, I knew you" (Jeremiah 1:5). Therefore, the life experiences that happened to us while we were in the womb can be viewed by God as occurring to us right now.

This matters because some of the wounds in clients' lives can begin as early as their days in utero. Research has shown that emotions of a mother can be passed on to an infant in her womb. If we were unwanted, or if our parents' world was filled with anger or anxiety or chaos, all those emotions can be trans-ferred to us, just as the toxic chemicals from tobacco or alcohol can be transferred to a growing fetus.

Learning this truth made me think of my own experience. About the time my mother became pregnant with me, two of her friends had given birth to malformed children. Their experience evoked deep fear in my mother that she, too, would give birth to a malformed baby. Her spirit of fear became mine, and as a boy, I was afraid of my own shadow.

However, during the time we helped Ruth re-experience her time in utero, what had been a deeply negative experience was transformed. During the prayer we asked her to relax and con-centrate on following the thoughts and words of the prayer into which we led her. Instead of the prayer time moving along like most intercession, the words of the prayer came slowly, with pauses for Ruth to assimilate what God was saying to her. We prayed along silently in support of her during these pauses, but also paid attention to her body language. Her eyes were closed but as the prayers continued her facial muscles relaxed, giving her a peaceful look. When she finally opened her eyes and was gently questioned, her experience fairly flowed out.

She described the sense of peace and healing that came to her as she allowed Jesus to re-create the first few months of her life in a way that was consistent with his Word and his love for her. "I was in a field with deep green grass, running, jumping and feeling bathed in the love of Jesus," she said. "In all my life I never experienced anything like this. The joy was overwhelming."

Not every client has a takeaway like Ruth's. For some the emotional experience is as transformational, but different pic-tures or thoughts come to mind. For some, the experience is more cognitive, with more of an intellectually based shift in how they describe their view of themselves.[1] But the bottom line is the same for those who are helped: instead of being locked into a self-

---

[1]Some cannot relate to the idea of Christ entering their journey at all the first time around; with these we may try later to re-introduce this kind of prayer.

esteem warped by others, the client is freed to take on what we call a God-esteem. They now see themselves as carefully created by God, and loved from the first moment of their existence.

Taking on emotional wounds with a self-concept weakened by a lifetime of blows is like sending a miniature poodle out to fight a Pit Bull. But going into the battle for healing armed with a strong experience of God-esteem provides strength and courage that will sustain your clients for the healing victories ahead.

Beginning the Session: Establishing Christ's Presence

Jesus promised that if two or three of us are gathered in his name, he is there, too (Matthew 18:20). That means Jesus himself is here with you and your client right now, ready to show his love and teach what's true. So, to begin the session, give him thanks for being present, and for the guidance and peace he brings. Bind any spirits of evil that may be present, and give them to Jesus for his disposal.

Prayer Focus: Re-entering Life from Your Conception

PRAYER MINISTER: Let your mind go back to the time before your conception. *Lord, clear [client's] mind from all distraction. Help [client] focus on your truth for her.*

God knew you, [client], from all eternity and set you apart for his purposes.
- *He tells you, "Before I formed you in the womb I knew you; before you were born I set you apart"* (Jeremiah 1:5).
- *"He chose (you) in him before the foundation of the world"* (Ephesians 1:4).

God planned for you to be born.
- *"You created my innermost being; you knit me together in my mother's womb," God's Word tells us* (Psalm 139:13).

God, please take [client] back to the time of her conception. No one knows this new life is beginning—only you and [client]— it is your shared secret. Father, shine your light, your presence and your peace into that womb. You are [client's] first and real parent. Please bathe your child in your warm, comforting oil.

Now, God, please draw out all feelings of anxiety, fear or rejection that may have come to her, and replace these negative feelings with your warm love, your peace. [PAUSE the prayer to allow time for the client to experience God's removal of the negative.]

May your Holy Spirit be a buffer between any negative thoughts, emotions or words of [client's] mother or father as they find out about the pregnancy. If these parents' response to the news led to her feeling unwanted or unloved, replace these feelings with your love, your peace.

Thank you, God, that you planned for [client] to be born. She was never a mistake. Bring to light any lies Satan has told her about her worth and confront these lies with your truth that [client] is "fearfully and wonderfully made," created by God himself, and that you have a purpose for her. [PAUSE the prayer to allow time for the client to experience God's assurance of purpose and worth.]

We now release [client] from any genetic problems, anything handed down through the generations—disease, anger, alcoholism, mental instability, lust, promiscuity, any sin or curses. By the power of your Spirit, we set her free. [PAUSE the prayer to allow time for the client to experience a sense of loosening from any evils.]

Holy Spirit, flow over [client's] sexuality with your anointing and blessing. Reassure her you wanted and planned for her to be a girl, a female (or a boy, male). Show her what a precious gift this is.

Now, as [client] continues to grow, to develop, inside her mother's womb, place within her all the gifting needed to become the special person you intended her to be. Bring your healing power into this time of growth to do exactly what needs to be done in [client's] life to perfectly form her for your holy purposes.

[PRAYER MINISTER: If appropriate, ask forgiveness for the parents who were so broken themselves that they couldn't see or love the great gift God was giving them in [client]. PAUSE to give time for the client to participate silently in this prayer.]

PRAYER MINISTER TO CLIENT - if life has been extremely difficult, you may ask: *"Are you able to ask Jesus to help you choose life?"* If the answer is yes,[2] move on to the time of the client's birth, and invite the client to picture herself emerging from the birth canal and seeing Jesus, waiting to welcome her with all his love and joy. Celebrate this moment with this prayer:

God, take us now to the time of [client's] birth. Remove any pain or trauma that may have attached to her. Let her birth be a time of great joy. May she know you are ready to receive her. You were so pleased that this was the time you determined from all eternity for [client] to come into this world. We ask now that she may be filled with your peace, power, love and encouragement. [PAUSE to allow client time to receive God's love and joy.]

Amen.

Concluding the Prayer Time

After the client has a time to quietly ponder this experience (watch body language), ask the client to share out loud what she experienced and how she feels now.

Whatever the experience, we like to end this session by sharing with the client a wonderful collection of Scriptures that bring to mind from God's Word who she truly is.

---

[2]Most clients answer yes, but if the answer is negative, ask, "If you knew that a loving God would go through all of life with you, helping you and redeeming you from all hurt, would you answer yes?" If their answer is still no, ask God to grace them to be able to say yes to life, to allow him to work in their lives and to bring healing to them so that they will want to experience a new life with him.

As you'll see, the self-image described through the 31 statements in *WHO AM I?* shines with the beauty and dignity afforded a true child of a King.

WHO AM I?

1. I am the salt of the earth (Matthew 3:13).
2. I am the light of the world (Matthew 5:14).
3. I am a child of God (John 1:12).
4. I am part of the true vine, a channel of Christ's life (John 15:1, 5).
5. I am Christ's friend (John 15:15).
6. I am chosen and appointed by Christ to bear his fruit (John 15:16).
7. I am a slave of righteousness (Romans 6:18).
8. I am enslaved to God (Romans 6:22).
9. I am a son of God; God is spiritually my Father (Galatians 3:26, 4:6).
10. I am a joint heir with Christ, sharing his inheritance with him (Romans 8:17).
11. I am temple, a dwelling place of God. His Spirit and his life dwell in me (I Corinthians 3:16, 6:19).
12. I am united to the Lord and am one spirit with him (I Corinthians 6:17).
13. I am a member of Christ's body (I Corinthians 12:27, Ephesians 5:30).
14. I am a new creation (II Corinthians 5:17).
15. I am reconciled to God and am a minister of reconciliation (II Corinthians 5:16, 19).
16. I am a son of God and one with Christ (Galatians 3:26, 28).
17. I am an heir of God since I am a son of God (Galatians 4:7).
18. I am a saint (Ephesians 1:1, I Corinthians 1:2, Philippians 1:1).

19. I am God's workmanship, his handiwork, born anew in Christ to do his work (Ephesians 2:10).
20. I am a fellow citizen with the rest of God's family (Ephesians 2:19).
21. I am righteous and holy (Ephesians 4:24).
22. I am a citizen of heaven, seated in heaven right now (Philippians 3:20, Ephesians 2:6).
23. I am hidden with Christ in God (Colossians 3:3).
24. I am chosen of God, holy and dearly loved (Colossians 3:12, I Thessalonians 1:4).
25. I am a son of light and not of darkness (I Thessalonians 5:5).
26. I am a holy partaker of a heavenly calling (Hebrews 3:1).
27. I am a partaker of Christ; I share in his life (Hebrews 3:14).
28. I am one of God's living stones, being built up in Christ as a spiritual house (I Peter 2:5).
29. I am a member of a chosen race, a royal priesthood, a holy nation, a people for God's own possession (I Peter 2:9,10).
30. I am an alien and stranger to this world in which I temporarily live (I Peter 2:11).
31. I am an enemy of the devil (I Peter 5:8-9).

If you plan to pray these prayers for someone else, it would be good to go through these verses in prayer and meditation first, to be able to understand and affirm them for yourself before you try to help others through them. When we present these Scriptures, we encourage clients to choose some of them that seem particularly meaningful. For these verses, we suggest they use this simple design to help guide their meditation:

1. Focus your mind on the meaning of this verse and what it implies for you.
2. Involving your feelings and will, make a commitment to change your life or thoughts to bring them into conformity with the insights God is giving you through this verse.
3. Pray for the Holy Spirit to give you the will and power to live out your commitment.

We're beginning now to help clients build a self-concept based on their worth and value to Almighty God, rather than the concept they acquired from the actions and opinions of those around them. A new way of seeing themselves has begun. This deepening connection to God's love and care for them provides a critical source of strength as we prepare to move in the next session toward forgiveness toward those who have wounded them.

Preparing for the Next Session:

For people who may have spent most of their lives feeling unwanted, useless or rejected, building a new, true picture of themselves as beloved, valuable and filled with purpose takes time. That's why a daily review of the WHO AM I? Scriptures is vital in helping the client prepare for the next—and most important—step toward deep, abiding healing, that of forgiving those who wounded them.

For some clients, experiences with an earthly father were very negative, either due to abuse or absence. To help make the shift from a disappointing father to a trustworthy one, and to see God as a loving Father who knows them personally and loves them deeply, we share a letter addressed to them from their heavenly Father. It begins, "My child..." and goes on in the warm, personal language of a true Father, to help them see themselves as he sees them, through eyes of love. We share this prayer with clients after this "Conception to Birth" session, as an additional resource to guide their meditation until we meet again. The letter reads like this:

My Child...

You may not know me, but I know everything about you (Psalm 139:1). I know when you sit down and when you rise up (Psalm 139:2). I am familiar with all of your ways (Psalm 139:3). Even the hairs on your head are numbered (Matthew 10:29-31). You were made in my image (Genesis 1:27). In me you live, move and have your being (Acts 17:28). You are my offspring (Acts 17:28). I knew you even before you were conceived (Jeremiah 1:4-5). I chose you when I planned creation (Ephesians 1:11-12). You were not a mistake (Psalm 139:15-16). All your days are written in my book (Psalm 139:15-16). I determined the exact time of your birth and where you would live (Acts 17:26). You are fearfully and wonderfully made (Psalm 139:14). I knit you together in your mother's womb (Psalm 139:13). I brought you forth on the day you were born (Psalm 71:6).

I have been misrepresented by those who know me (John 8:40-44). I am not distant or angry, but the complete expression of love (I John 4:16). My desire is to lavish my love on you, simply because you are my child and I am your Father (I John 3:1). I offer you more than your earthly father ever could (Matthew 7:11). I am the perfect Father (Matthew 5:48). Every good gift that you receive comes from my hand (James 1:17). I am your provider and I meet all your needs (Matthew 6:31-33). My plan for your future has always been filled with hope (Jeremiah 29:11). I love you with an everlasting love (Jeremiah 31:3). My thoughts toward you are as countless as the sand on the seashore (Psalm 139:17-18). I rejoice over you with singing (Zephaniah 3:17). I will never stop doing good to you (Jeremiah 32:40). You are my treasured possession (Exodus 19:5). I desire to establish you with all my heart and soul (Jeremiah 32:41). I want to show you great and marvelous things (Jeremiah 33:3). If you seek me with all of your heart you will find me (Deuteronomy 4:29). Delight in me and I will give you the desires of your heart (Psalm 37:4). It is I that gave you those desires (Philippians 2:13). I am able to do more for you than you could possibly imagine (Ephesians 3:20). I am your greatest encourager (II Thessalonians 2:16-17). I am also the Father who comforts you in all your troubles (II Corinthians 1:3-4). When you are brokenhearted, I am close to you (Psalm 34:18). As a shepherd carries a lamb, I carried you close to my heart (Isaiah 40:11). One day I will wipe away every tear from your eyes and I'll take away all the pain you suffered on this earth (Revelation 21:3-4).

I am your Father and I love you as I love my son, Jesus (John 17:23). In Jesus my love for you is revealed (John 17:26). He is the exact representation of my being (Hebrews 1:3). He came to demonstrate that I am for you, not against you (Romans 8:31). I am not counting your sins (II Corinthians 5:18-19). Jesus died so that you and I could be reconciled (II Corinthians 5:18-19). His death was the ultimate expression of my love for you (I John 4:10). I gave up everything that I loved so that I might gain your love (Romans 8:32). If you receive the gift of my son Jesus, you receive me (I John 2:23). Nothing will ever separate you from my love again (Romans 8:38-39).

Come home and I'll throw the biggest party heaven has ever seen (Luke 15:7). I have always been Father and will always be Father (Ephesians 3:14-15). My question is, will you be my child? (John 1:12-13). I am waiting for you (Luke 15:11-32).

Love, Your Dad, Almighty God

Forgiving Her Parents

Gertrude was a church member with multiple and deep wounds. She and her siblings were abandoned at an early age by alcoholic parents. Even though she was placed in a wonderful Christian foster home, she was plagued by questions about how her parents could leave her for alcohol, resulting in deep depression and suicidal thoughts. Later in life she actually attempted suicide several times.

After discussing the need to release her hurts to God and to forgive her parents, she prayed a very emotional prayer that produced a complete change in her attitude toward them.

When asked after the prayer how she felt, she replied, "If they walked into this room right now, I would run up to them, give them a big hug and tell them how much I loved them." This touch of Christ set the stage for a complete release from depression.

CHAPTER FIVE

Healing through Forgiving

*"If you hold anything against anyone, forgive him,
so that your Father in heaven may forgive you
your sins."*

MARK 11:25

Currently in the U.S. there are nearly four times as many lawyers as doctors. It may be that we care more about getting even than we do about getting well.

However, God sees this very differently. In his kingdom, getting well requires that we give up the right to get even, by forgiving those who have hurt us. His insistence on forgiveness comes with a very strong consequence for choosing another way. He said, "If you forgive men when they sin against you, your heavenly Father will also forgive you. But if you do not forgive men their sins, your Father will not forgive your sins" (Matthew 6:14-15).

Helping the wounded heal would be simpler if we could just nod our heads in agreement with Jesus' command, instruct our clients to declare forgiveness to their attackers, and move right on to inner healing. But praying with hundreds of clients has shown us how foolish such an approach would be. The deepest challenges to healing, in our experience, have come from our clients' struggles with forgiveness. At the same time, some of their greatest strides toward freedom and joy have resulted as they have ministered—and received—forgiveness.

The Challenge of Forgiveness

How hard should this be, really? One of the most widely perceived hallmarks of the Christian faith is forgiveness; even some non-Christians recognize Jesus' words on the cross, "Father, forgive them, for they know not what they do." Our prayer clients, particularly those with strong Christian backgrounds, tell us without hesitation, "I know I should forgive my enemies." The challenge with forgiveness isn't knowing what we should do; it's having the grace to do it when it simply, from a human perspective, feels so wrong.

Let me give you an example. When one of our clients, Susie, was four or five years old, her parents took her to a small lake surrounded by cypress trees draped in Spanish moss. For reasons I still can't comprehend, as her father rowed the boat to the middle of the lake, he began to describe to her all the terrible things in the water around them—poisonous snakes, hungry alligators and a whirlpool that would suck her under. He went on until it was clear his little daughter believed him, and was thoroughly terrified. Then he picked her up, threw her in the water, and rowed away! Her screams were met with mocking laughter. She was wearing a life jacket, so her abusive father could later say she wasn't in any danger, but to a little girl who believed and trusted those who were charged to care for her, the danger was life-threatening.

I'll confess. When I hear a story like this, my blood boils with the injustice of it. No child should ever be treated like this! And this experience is among the less horrific we've heard as we have entered the journeys of men and women with broken hearts. Now, we're about to turn to the woman who was once this child, and who has paid the price over a lifetime for treatment like this, and tell her she needs to forgive the one who did these things?

I hope you are able to feel the kinds of emotions an instruction like this can evoke with those we long to see set free. "Forgive him? Where is the justice in that? What he did was evil! And if I forgive him, what price does he pay for his actions? What defenses do I have going forward to keep him from hurting me again—it's my anger about these atrocities that give me strength!" We've heard all these responses, and more. We understand them. However, we cannot allow them to be the last word if these we care about are to see the healing and completion they seek.

Forgiveness Frees from the Prison of Bitterness

As prayer ministers, we can compassionately, gently, mercifully, but tenaciously help our clients move toward forgiveness if we are crystal clear on why it matters so deeply. We need to be equally clear on why a choice to live in bitterness matters just as deeply.

The Scripture is straightforward: unforgiveness shuts us off from grace, the heart of the gospel. The writer of Hebrews says it this way, "See that no one misses the grace of God, and that no bitter root grows up to cause trouble and defile many" (Hebrews 12:15). He makes three points about unforgiveness: first, like a root, it grows; it doesn't simply stay static. Second, it always causes trouble and defiles—a word that means "mar or spoil"—and third, it spreads its rottenness to others. Think of having a powerful acid in a container inside your body. Gradually the acid will eat through the walls of the container and destroy you from the inside out. When I hear some say they must retain bitterness as a way to get even with those who hurt them, I remember that bitterness is one of the few weapons that does far more harm to the person wielding it that it ever does to the enemy.

Let me illustrate. Sue walked with a limp because of a club foot. She'd had sixteen major surgeries, but was still living in constant pain. But we soon found that she was limping spiritually, too, because of bitterness. Sue was angry, angry at physicians who had botched some of the surgeries; angry at a church who didn't care for her; angry at her husband; angry at parents who had rejected her—The list went on, and I believe her complaints were legitimate. However, living under their control as she fed and nursed them wasn't legitimate for a deeply wounded woman who longed to live in joy. Through the course of our healing prayer sessions, Sue came to understand her need to forgive those who had hurt her, and took this courageous step of forgiving.

Interestingly, when we finished the forgiveness prayers, Sue left that session pain-free. She went on to a very successful foot surgery, and when we saw her a year later, she was walking without pain. (Notice that at no time did we pray for physical healing for her foot; it was the act of forgiveness that released her to receive this wonderful healing.) However, the more powerful point of her experience is this: Sue felt justified in harboring anger and bitterness, and perhaps she was. But her anger caused much more pain for herself than it ever did for others.

Another client, Jane, was so traumatized by a mother who had inflicted years of abuse that Jane would actually faint when she was in her mother's presence. When I first introduced the thought of forgiving her mother for the ways she had abused and abandoned her, Jane sat straight up in her chair and said, "That's impossible! It's not just that she lied to me and left me for eight years—she's still doing it and has no remorse." Jane needed time and experiences with God's healing before she could take this critical step of forgiving. But when she did—and even prayed blessing on her mother—she came to an immediate experience of spiritual renewal. She reported feeling "flooded with joy." The fainting spells stopped.

It's a paradox. To an outsider, forgiveness looks like giving up control and becoming weak and helpless. In reality, choosing to forgive our wounders puts us squarely in control. We are choosing to give them a gift they could never get on their own. The forgiver becomes one with the all-powerful King of Glory, who on the cross looked at those who had caused his suffering and said, "Father, forgive them." When we forgive, we do it in his power, and this new access to his power allows the door of the prison cell of darkness in which we've lived to swing open. We experience release from our binding to those who have hurt us, and walk in the light of God's freedom and health. (These benefits are now being documented in the psychological literature.[1])

The Path to Forgiveness

As we pray with clients for forgiveness, we walk with them through four important experiences. In the time of prayer, they will:

1. Forgive those who have wounded them
2. Ask forgiveness from God for the ways they may have hurt these wounders or harbored hatred toward them
3. Bless those who have wounded them
4. Ask for blessing for themselves.

Here is an example of what this prayer time might look like. One of the hurts Ruth brought centered on a deeply wounding experience in the fifth grade when her classmates—who had always demeaned and berated her—took advantage of a moment when the teacher stepped out of the classroom to join forces and ridicule her in a particularly humiliating way. Though being bullied wasn't new, this emotional beating from the whole class was unbearable; thoughts of it as an adult would send her into a panic. The scars she still bore from this experience had made her a loner who had great difficulty being in groups of people.

In the prayer time we asked her, as she described the hurt and the emotions she felt at the time, to place them in her outstretched hand. Then, she did the same with her own

---

[1]Witvliet, CVO (2001). Granting Forgiveness or Harboring Grudges: Implications for Emotions, Physiology and Health. (Psychological Science, Vol 12. No. 2, 117-123).

wrongdoing—that of hating these classmates for the pain they caused her. When she had finished, together we took these hurts and sins, and emptied her hands, emptied all of them at the foot of the cross. "I feel lighter and relieved," Ruth reported, "and peaceful." To seal this important transaction, she chose blessings to bestow on those classmates, and as she did, she picked up each one and placed it once again in her outstretched palm. Then she lifted her hands up to God and asked him to bless these classmates by his mercy and grace. She then chose blessings for herself, as well, and brought them to God.

Ruth's story illustrates three important pieces of the prayer of forgiveness.

First, it's critical that clients be specific about hurts and wounds they've experienced. A general statement like, "my father wasn't the dad he should have been," won't do. Second, emotions are as important as facts in this experience. It's tempting for clients to simply cognitively recount a moment of suffering, but work hard to suppress the pain it generated. To be free, emotions must, in the safety of this time of prayer, be reclaimed and felt. We watch carefully for body language that would suggest the client is actually feeling a measure of anger or distress as he or she names the hurtful moment. Third, the prayer of blessing for those who hurt them is crucial. We tell clients that being able to bless those who curse us is how we know forgiveness was real, and not just empty words. Surely blessing those who curse us is a supernatural act, rife with God's power and life!

Because this prayer has the ability to separate toxic emotions from the memory, at the conclusion of the prayer time we asked Ruth, "Would you go back to the memory and connect to the feelings you had at that time?" She did and told us, "I can connect to the feelings but they're not as strong as before." This is what healing sounds like. The memory of the act doesn't disappear, but its power to bind and hurt us fades away.

Ruth's experience was like that of Job. He suffered mightily at the hands of friends who, instead of offering comfort, blamed him for the hardships he experienced. When Job prayed blessings on these who had wounded him, God "restored his fortune—and then doubled it!" (Job 42:10-11 *The Message).*

Beginning the Session: Establishing Christ's Presence

When the Son of God came to share life with us, he brought a doorway to life eternal. He brought truth and light and rescue from our sins. But he also came to bring us healing. Doctor Luke, in his gospel, said of Jesus, "He began speaking to [the multitudes] about the kingdom of God and curing those who had need of healing" (Luke 9:11). He does this still today.

Invite the Holy Spirit, the agent of Christ's healing, to saturate each of you with his presence. Speak boldly to spirits of evil, in Jesus' name, commanding them as he did to leave. Finally ask God to draw out all your client's concerns—anything that might hinder from receiving the entire healing God has to offer—and replace them with his peace and comfort.

Prayer Focus: Four-Way Forgiveness Prayer

PRAYER MINISTER: We're about to pray what we call the "four-way forgiveness prayer." During this time you will both forgive, and seek forgiveness. When we pray, I'll ask you at different times to take hurts or sins and place them in your hands. Then, when we've finished, we'll release them to the Lord.

Step One: Hold up to the Lord all the things that trouble you [client] about the offender.

PRAYER MINISTER: Name each hurt out loud. Then pick up the hurt in one hand and place it in the other hand. Don't just say what the offender did to hurt you; it's critical that you also say how that offense made you feel. Put that feeling in your hand, along with the person's action. When you finish, put your hands together as a receptacle.

After client finishes, uplift the client's hands and pray this prayer slowly, with feeling:

Lord Jesus, we give you each of these things and ask you to take them and pour your love and healing through them. We thank you, Lord, that you have the power and the grace to redeem them. We ask you Lord to lift all the pain and hurt [client] has suffered from each of these—that you lift it from his mind, his heart and his spirit. We ask that you lift the burden of these things from his shoulders. We give all this to you, Lord, and we trust you to deal with them. Thank you, Lord, for taking each one of these things. Amen.

Allow time after the prayer for the deep healing to work *(watch body language).* After the prayer, ask the client "How are you feeling?"

Step Two: Hold up to the Lord all those things that trouble the offender about you (This step may not be applicable in instances of childhood victimization.)

PRAYER MINISTER: How have you offended the person you are forgiving? Speak out the sins you have committed against God regarding this person, one at a time, and mentally pick them up with one hand and place them in the other hand. When you finish, hold your hands together as we bring them to the cross of Jesus and I'll give a prayer. Remember you must be truly repentant of these sins before God. (In our society today individuals may be reluctant to identify thoughts of hatred, bitterness, vengeance, etc. as sins.)

When client finishes, again, take the client's hands and pray this prayer:

Lord Jesus, [client] comes to your cross, confessing sin against you and against [the offender]. He is truly sorry and asks your forgiveness. (Turn hands over, dumping out at cross, wiping clean.) Your blood runs over these sins, and we cut [client] free in the name of Jesus. We ask you to pour your love and healing power over these things. We ask you to take them, and we thank you for taking them, dealing with them and releasing this burden from [client]. We trust you to forgive [client] and to heal this hurt and pain. Amen.

Remember, God's Word says, "As far as the east is from the west, so far has he removed our transgressions from us" (Psalm 103:12). "Therefore, there is now no condemnation for those who are in Christ Jesus" (Romans 8:1).

Ask the client, "How are you feeling?"

Step Three: Hold up to the Lord your blessings for the offender.[2]

PRAYER MINISTER: Now, name the ways you wish God to bless [the offender]. As before, as you name each blessing, pick it up in one hand and place it in the other hand. When you're finished, put your hands together and lift them to God's throne.

When completed, pray this prayer:

Lord, we give [the offender] to you. We thank you that you are able to handle him better than anyone else. Bring about your perfect will for him and let your love pour into, and your healing power flow over him. We release [the offender] into your care. Amen.

Step Four: Hold up to the Lord your blessings for yourself.

PRAYER MINISTER: What would you like Jesus to do in your life today? How would you like God to bless you? Speak out each blessing, place it into your hand, and then hold your hands together and lift them up to God.

---

[2]Since this prayer is released to God for him to deal with in all his mercy and compassion, it can be prayed even if the offender is deceased. It is the client's hurtful memory that we are focusing on and his willfully praying a blessing on the offender is an important aspect of his healing.

Upon completion, pray this prayer:

Lord, we release these things to you and ask that you pour your love, mercy and grace into them. We thank you that [client] trusts you with these things. Surround him with your heavenly angels. Help him to know you and how much you love him. Amen.

Concluding the Prayer Time

After forgiving and asking forgiveness, you've asked the client about feelings. Because of God's promise to forgive our sins when we confess them, and then to cleanse us of all unrighteousness, your client has come into a new place of lightness and freedom in Christ. Praise God!

During the week ahead, your client will be encouraged to experiment with a different approach to meditation. For those who might be more intuitive or subjective in their personalities, this approach can bring a rich and lively encounter with God's truth. Encourage your client to choose a Scripture or two daily and meditate on it deeply, using the format offered below as a guide.

A Meditation Experience

1. *Preparation:* Let your imagination roam, place yourself in the presence of God, affirming that since God is everywhere, he is here now. Think of Christ as standing at your side, sharing your experience. Offer a prayer of confession and request guidance in the meditation to follow.
2. *Consideration:* Propose a subject, perhaps suggested by a Bible verse you just read, and focus your mind on that subject.
3. *Resolution:* Involve your feelings and your will. How should your life change as a result of what you have considered? Resolve to make those changes accordingly, with God's help.

4. *Conclusion:* Offer a prayer of thanksgiving for what you have learned, of consecration for what you intend to change, or petition for grace and strength to fulfill the resolution.

Scriptures for Meditation

1. Matthew 11:28 - "Come to me, all you who are weary and burdened, and I will give you rest."
2. Jeremiah 1:5 - "Before I formed you in the womb I knew you, before you were born I set you apart."
3. Psalm 139:13 - "For you created my inmost being; you knit me together in my mother's womb."
4. Isaiah 49:15-16 - "Can a mother forget the baby at her breast and have no compassion on the child she has borne? Though she may forget, I will not forget you! See, I have engraved you on the palms of my hands."
5. Philippians 4:6-7 - "Do not be anxious about anything, but in everything, by prayer and petition, with thanksgiving, present your requests to God. And the peace of God, which transcends all understanding, will guard your hearts and your minds in Christ Jesus."
6. James 4:7-8a - "Submit yourselves, then, to God. Resist the devil, and he will flee from you. Come near to God and he will come near to you."
7. II Timothy 1:7 - "For God did not give us a spirit of timidity, but a spirit of power, of love and of self-discipline."
8. Philippians 4:13 - "I can do everything through him who gives me strength."
9. Nehemiah 8:10b - "The joy of the Lord is your strength."
10. Psalm 34:4 - "I sought the Lord, and he answered me; he delivered me from all my fears."
11. Psalm 91:1-2 - "He who dwells in the shelter of the Most High will rest in the shadow of the Almighty. I will say of the Lord, 'He is my refuge and my fortress, my God, in whom I trust.'"

12. Psalm 5:3 - "In the morning, O Lord, you hear my voice; in the morning I lay my requests before you and wait in expectation."

13. I John 4:4b - "The one who is in you is greater than the one who is in the world."

14. I Peter 5:7-9 - "Cast all your anxiety on him because he cares for you. Be self-controlled and alert. Your enemy the devil prowls around like a roaring lion looking for someone to devour. Resist him, standing firm in the faith."

15. Isaiah 41:10,13 - "So do not fear, for I am with you; do not be dismayed, for I am your God. I will strengthen you and help you; I will uphold you with my righteous right hand. For I am the Lord, your God, who takes hold of your right hand and says to you, 'Do not fear; I will help you.'"

16. Isaiah 43:1-3 - "But now, this is what the Lord says—he who created you, O Jacob, he who formed you, O Israel: 'Fear not, for I have redeemed you; I have summoned you by name; you are mine. When you pass through the waters, I will be with you; and when you pass through the rivers, they will not sweep over you. When you walk through the fire, you will not be burned; the flames will not set you ablaze. For I am the Lord, your God, the Holy One of Israel, your Savior; ... you are precious and honored in my sight, and I love you.'"

17. Romans 15:13 - "May the God of hope fill you with all joy and peace as you trust in him, so that you may overflow with hope by the power of the Holy Spirit."

18. Psalm 66:18 - "If I had cherished sin in my heart, the Lord would not have listened."

Preparing for the Next Session:

Next week, we'll be moving to a deeper experience of inner healing. You've been faithful to clear away the barriers to healing; now God is free to touch you even more deeply. This week, rejoice in his love for you, and give thanks for the healing you've experienced so far. Tell him how much you love him, and enjoy being his child!

Clear Changes

Betty reported clear before-and-after changes from healing prayer.

She had married an abusive alcoholic, and since divorced. During prayer, she forgave him. "I wouldn't marry him again," she told us, "but I have forgiven him."

Socially she was timid and shy, always feeling like others saw an oddball when they looked at her. After prayer, she bought herself a mug that trumpeted "World's Greatest Bookkeeper." "I don't think it's pride," she said, "it's just that now it's okay to feel good about myself."

Before prayer she'd regularly made sure her hair looked nice when she went to bed, because she so feared for her daughters' safety that she expected a call from the police or hospital telling her something terrible had happened. Prayer helped her stop taking an antidepressant, and to rest well.

CHAPTER SIX

Going Deeper into Inner Healing

"I pray that...Christ will make his home in your hearts as you trust in him."

EPHESIANS 3:16-17 (TLB)

My wife Eleanor and I are both of Dutch descent, and as you may know, the Dutch have a reputation for tidiness. If you came into our home, I hope you'd see some of that tidiness evidenced. But I'd also be glad that your good manners would prevent you from checking too closely, especially when it came to the closets.

This session of healing prayer is an emotional "closet cleaning." Paul encourages us in Ephesians 3:17 to invite Christ to become at home in our lives. In the healing prayers we've practiced so far, he has had opportunity to move into major places where previously bitterness or pain had barred his entry. But our deepest joy will come when he is offered opportunity to move into *every* part of the home that is our inner life—not just every major room, but every storage room and closet, as well. "At-home-ness" with Christ means there's nothing we have to hide; no place we fear he will stumble upon; no cupboard we must keep locked so he won't open the door.

As we work with prayer clients, we find these locked closets in the form of hurts that didn't heal in previous prayer sessions. Though they typically have found some measure of freedom and peace by this time in the relationship, for many there lingers a wound, or perhaps several wounds, that still have power to generate great pain. We are identifying these persistent wounds when we ask, perhaps after the Forgiveness Prayer, what the client has felt. When a memory still has pain associated with it, we know more work needs to be done because it isn't actually the memory that limits their lives; it's the pain.

Here's what I mean. Think back to what you've heard about veterans of military combat who suffer from Post-Traumatic Stress Disorder (PTSD). You may be standing next to them, and a helicopter flies over—to you it's simply a helicopter, and you wonder if someone's being life-flighted to the hospital or if a traffic accident has taken place. You're interested and curious, but that's the extent of your reaction. But a PTSD sufferer may hear something very different in the whir of the helicopter. One high school principal who was a Viet Nam combat veteran said, "I was once in an auto body shop, and a helicopter went over. Without even realizing what I was doing, I hit the floor. Of course I was terribly embarrassed when I came to my senses, but that sound meant only one thing to me—I was under attack and in terrible danger. When I got up, my heart was pounding, my breath came in gasps, and all my systems were on high-alert." This man's years in combat had turned what should have been a non-threatening sound into an emotionally charged trigger for trauma, and he responded as if there were actually a clear and present danger.

This is how persistent, wounding memories work for some of our clients. A friend's comment, a movie scene, a holiday like Mother's Day can be the trigger that brings back, not just a memory, but a debilitating rush of pain or anxiety that can cause an otherwise normal-looking person to "hit the deck" emotionally. One of our clients, Nicole, "hit the deck" when

she sat with us, watching a training video for prayer ministers. I commented in the video that it's hard to understand and
believe the love of God the Father if we lacked a father's love
as we grew up. Nicole began to cry, and actually pulled herself
into a fetal-like ball in the corner of the sofa. Her sobbing went
on for several minutes. That fathering reminder, heard in a
setting that was safe enough to allow her to feel her own pain,
triggered an emotional outburst that surprised all of us with
its intensity. Our goal, then, with Nicole was not to erase the
memories of her past—some would suggest that may not even
be possible—but to disconnect the negative emotions associated with those memories. When this happens, these memories become simply mind-pictures, not binders or drivers of
depression and anxiety. It's helping with these deeper and
more persistent wounds we're going to address through the
prayer experience called Inner Healing.

The Truths That Support Inner Healing

This prayer experience appropriates what I call the "Great
Exchange" God planned between Jesus and ourselves. Here's
what I mean. Jesus, the Sinless One, took on sin so we sinful
ones could take on his righteousness (II Corinthians 5:21).
Jesus, the Complete One, took on wounds so we wounded and
broken ones could receive his health and completion (Matthew
8:17). What a glorious, but completely unequal, exchange! How
God loves us to make such an exchange possible! Since Christ is
bringing all the righteousness and health and completion of God
to this exchange, how foolish we would be to refuse to let go of
our sins and wounds to accept his fullness. John celebrates this
truth when he says of Jesus, "From the fullness of his grace we
all received one blessing after another" (John 1:16). Prayer for
Inner Healing provides a way for all the grace and blessing necessary to heal the deepest wounds to be administered to those
who ache with grief and pain.

The second truth that drives the Prayer for Inner Healing is one we've already discussed, that of God's eternal timelessness. Because sequential time as we experience it doesn't apply to the One who "was, and is, and is to come" (Revelation 4:9), he is able to join us right now in events that in our view of life happened in the past. In the Prayer for Inner Healing, we can experience him there, and find his grace to stop a river of pain in our lives at its very mouth, before it gets a chance to claim our lives. God's timelessness makes possible a "holy do-over," getting to start again. We saw the power of this in the Conception-to-Birth Prayer, and now we are going to draw on this same truth about God to empower and fill the **Prayer for Inner Healing**.

Beginning the Session: Establishing Christ's Presence

Begin your prayer time today giving thanks for the Great Exchange—the Holy One became unholy so we could be holy; the Unblemished One took on brokenness so we could be made whole. Thank him for both his heart and power to heal us. And speak boldly to spirits of evil that want to keep us broken and in pain. Bind them in Jesus' dear name, and by his authority, leave them with Jesus for his disposal. This is a holy time and a holy place. Ask the Holy Spirit to bring his peace and power so the healing God intends can flow.

Prayer Focus:

PRAYER MINISTER: Today we're going to invite Jesus to join you in the moments of deepest wounding in your life. As you recall places where you still feel deep sorrow or hurt, we'll re-enter these with Jesus and let him re-create these moments in ways that set you free of their weight.

Close your eyes, and go back to the painful memory. Enter into those feelings you experienced at that time; stay connected

to the feelings, and don't offer any prayers to God. Are you connected to the feelings? (Pause for answer.)

I'm going to ask God to come into your memory at the time
the event occurred, and provide his healing. Then I'll wait here
with you quietly, supporting you in prayer. When God has completed his work or when you feel you are ready, you can open
your eyes, and I'll know you are finished.

Prayer: *Jesus, come now into this painful moment with
[client]. Feel it with her and minister your healing in the way she
can best receive it.*

INSTRUCTION to PRAYER MINISTER: Pray quietly in your
mind or in the Spirit while you sit with the client. Watch for
clues from her body language, and when it appears some change
has taken place, you might ask gently, "What are you experiencing?" Or, when the client opens her eyes, that same question is
in order.

If the client reports that nothing happened, you will offer
a prayer to bind up any spirits of evil that may be hindering the
healing.

*In the authority of Jesus' name, I now bind any forces of evil
which may be attempting to hinder this healing work of Christ
for (client).*

Then, repeat the initial Prayer for Inner Healing. In our
study, this intervention has been effective in most cases.

Possible Responses

As you'll recall from previous sessions, Ruth had experienced
genuine moments of healing and release. But in the case of one
memory, that of the humiliating bullying she received from a
large group of schoolmates, the pain didn't totally release. So,
we met this memory with the Prayer for Inner Healing.

As we began the prayer, we told Ruth, "Go back to that
traumatic classroom memory. Connect with your emotions in
that situation and just stay there as best you can. Don't pray

or attempt to imagine anything; just stay in the memory and emotions with your eyes closed. During this time, we will pray a simple prayer asking God to come into that classroom with his healing presence. When God is finished working, or if nothing happens, open your eyes."

As we sat quietly praying, tears began forming in Ruth's eyes. "She's in the memory and connected to her emotions," I thought. After a while, the tension in her face eased and her body seemed to relax. She opened her eyes, and I asked, "What did God do?"

She responded, "I was in the classroom. The kids were poking fun at me, and I felt awful. Then all of a sudden I began laughing and everyone was smiling and laughing *with* me. When I started walking, full of joy, out of the classroom, the experience faded." We invited her to take a few moments and bask in this new memory and the positive new feelings it evoked. Then we asked her to return to the hurtful memory and connect with the emotions. "The hurt is gone," she said immediately. "I can bring up the memory, but now it's associated with a warm feeling." We told Ruth to journal this experience, as we tell all our clients. It's important for them to document the things God has done for them and their response to God's healing intervention. This can be healing in itself.

For Susie, the experience was somewhat different, but still powerful. Susie, as you may recall, was the little girl thrown in what she thought was an alligator-filled lake by her father, then left. Though she saw progress in other issues during healing prayer, this particular memory still haunted her. And, it generated a question she repeated again and again in our sessions. "I don't understand it," she shook her head. "How could a loving God allow such a hurtful thing to happen to me? When I get to heaven, that's the first question I'm going to ask him."

During this Prayer for Inner Healing she sat with eyes closed for a long time. When she finally opened her eyes, she told us about feeling the horror of that moment. But then, Jesus came to her, took her in his arms, and told her, "Everything will be all right."

I left time for this wonderful experience to soak in, and finally said, "Susie, did you ask Jesus your question?" She smiled. "Oh, no. It was so wonderful and I felt so much love and peace that the question just went away."

Nicole was repeatedly beaten and molested in a series of foster families. Like Ruth, she saw great healing in prayer, starting with the Conception to Birth Prayer. But some of her wounds were so deep-seated, it took the Prayer of Inner Healing to reach a place of freedom. Her experience with this prayer was so deep and abiding, that she recorded it in her own words.

My adoptive family was hardest to forgive. The week before this [Prayer for Inner Healing] session I fought with everyone in my path. I didn't read my Bible verses or prayers, and that made the week even worse. But even though my stomach hurt, I climbed the wooden steps to the prayer room again, and we began. Peter prayed that Satan's powers would be bound and that God's love would fill the room and me.

Eleanor prayed that the Lord would take me back to my tenth year and provide healing. We sat silently, and then I was in the Spirit in the house where I had been adopted at 10.

I saw Satan—in the form of both my mother and my brother. They chased me through the hallway shouting, "You are trash. It was born and bred into you. You will never amount to nothin'! No one wants you, not even your real mother."

In my heart I heard, "This is not true. Do not believe it."

I cried out, "Jesus!" But I couldn't see him.

I ran from room to room looking for him—living room, kitchen, the hallway to the bedrooms. I skipped the bedrooms themselves—they were where I had been beaten most often.

"Where is Jesus?" I wondered. He was with me in all the other times of healing prayers.

I ran through the rooms and to the hallway screaming, "Jesus, where are you?" Memories of everything that happened there followed me. Finally, I got the courage and ran through the bedrooms. I found him in mine. He was locked in the corner of my room behind a small, translucent baby gate. "Grab my hand, and let's get out of here," I said.

"I can't," he answered.

I asked why.

He pointed to the baby gate. This was the corner where I would go to curl up and cry after a beating. It was here I had given up on God. I had locked Jesus away from my life. I had locked his power in the corner of my bedroom, and I needed to let him out. I opened the gate. He walked with me through memories of some of the worst beatings, each time being there with me, even the time my mother almost killed me. I saw myself in the corner facing her with the broken broom handle coming toward me. I saw him grab me by the hands, pull me through her legs and lead me to the door. He had been there with me—I just hadn't seen him!

I walked through the door and through every room. Each one we entered filled with his glowing light.

When we came to my brother's room, he was there. I faced my brother with Jesus holding my hand, and I told him, "You cannot hurt me anymore." He vanished.

At the front door my mother grabbed me in the old head-lock. "You can't hurt me any more because I belong to Jesus," I said. Jesus pulled me free, and we walked down the sidewalk together. I looked back. She looked so small and so weak. Holding Jesus' hand, I felt strong.

At the driveway I looked back at the house and asked, "Can we burn it?"

Jesus lifted his finger and the house burst into giant flames. Then he reached down and stripped off a giant black scab that covered my whole back. He threw it to the ground, and I knew I was finally free of her. She could no longer hurt me. And I could love her in a right way. A love through the power of God replaced the desperate, needy love of my childhood.

When I told Peter and Eleanor that Jesus had finished reveal-
ing himself to me in my adoptive home, we prayed together. I
forgave my adoptive family, and we prayed blessings on my
mother and my brother—and on my father, too. He had been
gone so much of the time, he had been blind to what had been
happening with the three of us. I prayed for God to forgive me
too, for hating them and for giving up on him. I had shut my eyes
to Jesus but he had saved me from mother's broken broomstick
and led me to safety.

We asked for God to bless me, too. And he did. One bless-
ing he gave was the blessing of growing up. Until now I had felt
trapped as a scared little 10-year-old girl who couldn't hold her
head up or feel as if she belonged. She was out of place wherever
she went. Emotionally, I had remained a 10-year-old girl. Now,
for the first time in my life, I began to feel like an adult. A fresh
new world of womanhood opened up before me.

These three clients had clearly identifiable encounters with
Jesus, and it happens this way for many. However, not everyone
experiences him the same way. For some there is simply a new
feeling of peace. For others, a Bible verse comes to mind, and
gives them insight or comfort.

Some clients have no response at all. We believe the lack
of response may be the result of demonic interference. After
prayers to bind up evil, there is most often healing in a second
session of prayer.

Concluding the Prayer Time

Experiencing the touch of Jesus in place of long-term shame
and brokenness can be powerful, indeed. It is natural for love
and joy to flow freely, and for the Word of God to take on a new
attraction. This week you may want to introduce the idea of
"praying the Scripture" as a way to meditate on God's Word. It is
a simple tool, but often brings fresh life to Scriptures that now
may have new meaning. Encourage your client to read the list of

Scriptures provided (see Appendix for more), and mark several that seem to have special meaning to them. Then, encourage them to take each verse and re-create it as a prayer.

For example, John 10:10 says, "The thief comes only to steal and kill and destroy; I [Jesus] have come that they may have life, and life to the full." To pray this Scripture, a client might say, "*Jesus, the thief who steals, kills and destroys wanted to do all these things to me. Thank you for stopping him. Thank you that your desire for me is just the opposite—your will for me is life that's full, not empty. Living with you I lack nothing. I love living with you and experiencing you filling up every part of my heart and life. Thank you!*"

Further Scriptures for Meditation

19. Romans 8:1 - "Therefore, there is now no condemnation for those who are in Christ Jesus."
20. Jeremiah 29:11 - "For I know the plans I have for you," declares the Lord, "plans to prosper you and not to harm you, plans to give you hope and a future."
21. Jeremiah 29:12-13 - "Then you will call upon me and come and pray to me, and I will listen to you. You will seek me and find me when you seek me with all your heart."
22. Isaiah 30:21 - "Whether you turn to the right or to the left, your ears will hear a voice behind you, saying, 'This is the way; walk in it.'"
23. Philippians 2:12b-13 - "Continue to work out your salvation with fear and trembling, for it is God who works in you to will and to act according to his good purpose."
24. Philippians 1:6 - "Being confident of this, that he who began a good work in you will carry it on to completion until the day of Christ Jesus."
25. Ephesians 4:26-27 - "'In your anger do not sin': Do not let the sun go down while you are still angry, and do not give the devil a foothold."

26. Romans 8:38-39 - "For I am convinced that neither death nor life, neither angels nor demons, neither the present nor the future, nor any powers, neither height nor depth, nor anything else in all creation, will be able to separate us from the love of God that is in Christ Jesus our Lord."

27. II Corinthians 10:5b - "We take captive every thought to make it obedient to Christ."

28. Galatians 5:1 - "It is for freedom that Christ has set us free. Stand firm, then, and do not let yourselves be burdened again by a yoke of slavery."

29. John 8:32 - "Then you will know the truth, and the truth will set you free."

30. John 3:34b - "God gives the Spirit without limit."

31. I John 1:9 - "If we confess our sins, he is faithful and just and will forgive us our sins and purify us from all unrighteousness."

32. Galatians 5:24-25 - "Those who belong to Christ Jesus have crucified its sinful nature with its passions and desires. Since we live by the Spirit, let us keep in step with the Spirit."

33. Romans 12:2a - "Do not conform any longer to the pattern of this world, but be transformed by the renewing of your mind."

34. I Corinthians 2:16b - "But we have the mind of Christ."

35. I Corinthians 15:57-58 - "Thanks be to God! He gives us the victory through our Lord Jesus Christ. Therefore, my dear brothers, stand firm. Let nothing move you. Always give yourselves fully to the work of the Lord, because you know that your labor in the Lord is not in vain.

36. Philippians 4:4-5 - "Always be full of joy in the Lord. I say it again—rejoice! Let everyone see that you are considerate in all you do. Remember, the Lord is coming soon" (NLT).

37. Philippians 4:8b - "Fix your thoughts on what is true and honorable and right. Think about things that are pure and lovely and admirable. Think about things that are excellent and worthy of praise."

Preparing for the Next Session:

What we've discussed so far represents a fairly typical healing prayer relationship. Most of the time when we prayed with people, we moved through the sequence you've just read about and found they experienced a healing encounter with God that met their needs in a deep way.

However, not every client fits this pattern. There are several situations that call for discernment and somewhat different interventions. We'll look at some of these together.

May I close with a word of encouragement? Some may feel that just because praying with others for healing isn't a cut-and-dried process, with an inflexible set of steps to follow, they may "make a mistake" or "do it wrong." Nothing could be further from the truth because God does not send us alone or unequipped into this work. The Holy Spirit, whose assignment from the Father is to guide us into all truth, is always present—because each week you invite him to be present—and provides wisdom and confidence to know how best to support your client. It is his partnership, leading and presence that allow us to participate in this holy ministry of reconciliation, and all we need to minister in his name will be ours, just at the moment we need it. Our assignment is to remain whole with the Lord ourselves, no known sin hindering us.

Walls Coming Down

Martha complained of unexplained headaches and a burning on the side of her face. She suspected demonic influence since the symptoms only came when she was in church.

Her parents divorced when she was in junior high; she could recall her mother leaving with a suitcase. "But I didn't—I don't—feel anything with that memory, " she said. However, as an adult, she described herself as "standoffish" and not affectionate. She felt as though her church had a wall around it, keeping her on the outside. During prayer, she began to release feelings she didn't know were there—and shed many tears. There was a wall, but it was one she had put around herself to protect from hurt. Through prayer, both the wall and the headaches and burning disappeared.

CHAPTER SEVEN

Removing Strongholds of Evil

*"He is my loving God and my fortress, my
stronghold and my deliverer, my shield, in whom I
take refuge."*

PSALM 43:2

When we've reached this point in the prayer journey, clients
should have experienced a touch of Christ—perhaps many
times—as we brought their hurts to the Healer. But sometimes
there are pains so deeply embedded in our spirits and our
psyches that final barriers must be removed before these hurts
can be released.

I think of it like this. When Jesus entered a village called
Bethsaida, townspeople brought a blind man to him, begging
Christ to heal him. So the Lord took the man by the hand and
led him outside the village. In an interesting variation on his
approach to healing, Jesus spit on the man's eyes, put his hands
on them, and then asked him, "Do you see anything?" The man
replied, "I see people; they look like trees walking around." So
Jesus once more put his hands on the man's eyes. "Then," the
Scripture records, "His eyes were opened, his sight was restored,
and he saw everything clearly" (Mark 8:22-25).

I don't know all the implications of what this encounter was meant to teach us, but I do know this: sometimes it takes more than one prayer experience for total healing to be demonstrated. In our experience with praying for inner healing, we find the healing progression often works like this:

1. Four-Way Forgiveness Prayer: *A large percentage of hurts are released.*
2. Prayer for Inner Healing: *Deeper hurts are released.*
3. Additional Prayers for Unresolved Issues: *Further healing takes place.*

We'll explore together some of these unresolved issues that can stand in the way of the deepest healing, and then learn to apply the prayers that speak to these barriers. Ones we deal with most commonly are:

1. Inhibiting Vows or Promises
2. Unnurtured Spirit
3. Strongholds of Satan

You may, as we often do, use one or more of these prayers in additional healing prayer sessions. If you do, of course you'll want to begin as you have consistently, by sharing a prayer with the client that invites the Holy Spirit to be present with his power and grace, and binding spirits of evil that want to hinder this magnificent work.

The Barrier of Destructive Vows or Promises

When children live in a dysfunctional, abusive environment, they often make vows to themselves about how they will be different when they grow up.

Our client Ruth, whom you have come to know well by now, could recollect many of her vows. Growing up, men came and went from her family; most of her siblings had different fathers. In reaction to this chaos, Ruth vowed that when she married, she would never leave. She promised herself she would never be violent or abusive. And, her experiences of abandonment caused her to promise herself she would never let anyone see how she hurt. She would never be weak or trust anyone.

It's easy to understand how promises like this made sense to the abused child Ruth had been. However, in her adult life, they played out in ways that made her life much harder. For example, though being faithful in marriage "'til death do us part" is very important, in Ruth's case it left her paralyzed when the man she married became cruel and abusive. "I'm very afraid of him," she told us, "but I cannot leave him. I can't." With her children there were negative consequences of her vows, as well, because by her own admission, "I have a terrible time trying to discipline them." Her vow to never be violent or abusive was binding her from making reasonable choices about providing consequences for her children's misbehavior. Also, vowing to never show weakness resulted in enough discomfort around others that eventually she wound up lonely and relationally isolated.

Vows like the ones Ruth made shut God out. We have determined how we will or will not live life. We become our own sources of guidance and wisdom. So much for the Holy Spirit and his leadership in our lives! What we crafted as a defense against further hurts becomes a prison that locks us inside, limiting God's ability to lead us, guide us, give us his wisdom and teach us his truth. (In the next session, "Staying Healthy," we'll explore more deeply how to help clients replace destructive promises with thoughts, words and beliefs that are congruent with God's truth and reinforce, rather than weaken, the inner healing they've received.)

Here are some examples of **Inner Vows**. We find this list useful in helping clients identify places in their lives in which they've made vows that now bind them.

I will never:

- Let anyone love me
- Be weak

- Trust anyone
- Allow myself to need
- Let them take anything away from me
- Allow anyone to touch me
- Share what is mine
- Allow anyone to give me money
- Allow myself to be hit
- Go out at night
- Let anyone see who I am
- Let anyone know I hurt
- Tell a woman (or man) anything
- Let a man (or woman) control me
- Be responsible for the actions of others
- Receive a compliment
- Participate in life
- Allow a woman (or man) into my heart
- Be anything worthwhile
- Be sick
- Be violent or abusive
- Grow up, mature
- Forgive [_____]

I will always:

- Remain aloof, separate
- Be logical
- Be in control of my life

The most important inner vow is this: "I will never raise my children as my mother (or father) raised me." This one is the most deep-seated and damaging in most people and must be dealt with. Why? Ephesians 6:2 tells us to honor our father and mother. It doesn't say, "Honor your father and your mother *if they act honorably to you.*" Holding unforgiveness in our hearts handicaps us in life. Your client may have forgiven parent(s) in the Four-way Forgiveness Prayer, but vows bind at a deeper level.

Living out a vow allows Satan into our lives. We are running our own lives, not going to God to guide us.

Instead of living controlled by vows like these, clients need to choose a life controlled by God. When we pray with clients to break destructive vows that have hindered them, we do so after they have forgiven the people who had wounded them. Also, negative emotions connected to these wounds have been separated from the memories by the Prayer of Inner Healing. With these foundational healings already in place, they are ready to take this step toward a life freer from barriers to joy and health.

Prayer Focus:

CLIENT: *I renounce these vows:* [name specifically].

PRAYER MINISTER: *By the power and authority of Jesus, I break these vows. I command your spirit and body to no longer remember them. You are free, restored to your original design. You are no longer required to feel, think and act according to these vows. In the name of our Lord Jesus Christ, I ask for protection, peace and comfort for you and your family. Amen.*

Prayer Reinforcement:

As we have seen, Ruth came to this session living out certain vows her entire life. They were identified, and a prayer said to break their power. However, they remained deeply imbedded in the way she thought and functioned. To remove them completely required focused, attentive work on her part, cooperating with the enabling power of God. We instructed her to identify the thought patterns and actions she had practiced as she lived under the power of these vows. Going forward, we encouraged her to visualize a stop sign every time one of these thought patterns or actions occurred, and then say to God, *"I know where this is coming from. God, how do **you** want me to think, act or react?"*

At first she found herself repeating this prayer many times a day. However, over time, these old thoughts and actions were replaced by new ones. Ruth gradually developed the thoughts of Christ (see in appendix - **Breaking Strongholds through Prayer**).

For example, Ruth had a deep fear of her husband that prevented honest communication and an open sharing of feelings. To counteract these fears she could now address them using what she had been taught in previous sessions—the meditation of Scriptures that counteracted these fears. As she did this, she became God's person who could speak not her words but God's words in love to her husband.

The Barrier of the Unawakened Self

Many of our clients had their first and most powerful experiences of wounding early in their lives, and far too many suffered at the hands of their father, mother, or other primary caretaker. These wounds to ones so vulnerable who are just beginning to learn self-concepts and life patterns can lead to two destructive patterns we often see, and these defenses go very deep. The first is what we call "the heart of flesh," protections built early and solidly to keep others from getting close, since closeness meant pain.

The other is what we call a "slumbering spirit." One of parents' primary redemptive roles in their children's development is to call them to life—to make life and living so positive, safe and inviting, that children want to mature into adulthood. Children called to life feel a general sense of anticipation and hope as they enter each day, and expect good, rather than evil, to be their lot in life. This "call to life" is often silenced in children of abuse, but God is well able, in his healing power, to re-issue the call, and to bring them into the confidence and vitality that makes daily life a joy. To speak to this need, we use a prayer called "**Slumbering Spirits.**"[1]

---

[1]These prayers do not mean that clients must now seek out the offending party to build a new relationship. God must lead them. In some cases, a wonderful

Prayer Focus:[2]

Prayer for a Heart of Flesh: (Ezekiel 36:26)

CLIENT reads aloud in presence of PRAYER MINISTER:

Lord, I have developed a defense to keep myself from being seen. I have built a hiding place to protect myself from hurt. I know this "protection" blocks the love, warmth and nurturing for which I long. I come to you, Lord, because I am helpless to change. I invite you into my life to take down the wall. I want you to be my defense. Lord, help me to become vulnerable, to risk love.

Lord, I forgive those people who have wounded me, and I forgive you, Lord, for allowing these wounds into my life. I also forgive myself for the sinful reactions to hurt and for building this heart of stone.

Father, please forgive me for my sinful responses and for the ways I have hurt loved ones by keeping them out of my life. I repent for the destruction in my own life and for wounding you with my sin. Please forgive me.

Lord, as an act of my will I choose to be connected to others within the body of Christ and within my family. I want to be intimate. Forgive me, Lord, for not trusting the love offered me by my spouse, children and fellow Christians. Help me to see and appreciate the gifts of others. Put a watch on my lips that I may build up instead of tear down. Help me hear warnings or rebukes as love and not rejection. Help me hold myself in the vulnerable position of receiving ministry, not just offering it. I ask you to bring those people into my life who know how to love uncon-ditionally and still have courage to hold me accountable. Bring

---

relationship follows; in others, it is best to stay away. They must ask God for his guidance in this.

[2]In the following prayers, the clients, of necessity, must comprehend what they are reading. The Prayer Minister may ask if the client sees himself in the previ-ous paragraph. If appropriate, the Prayer Minister may read the prayer slowly, by paragraph, for the client, discussing it as necessary.

to death my heart of stone and give me a heart of flesh (a new, obedient heart).

In Jesus' name I pray, Amen.

Prayer to Awaken Slumbering Spirits:

CLIENT reads aloud in presence of PRAYER MINISTER:

Thank you, Father God, that at my conception you breathed life into me. You created me to be one with you and to have fellowship with you, my spirit to your Spirit. Lord, come and minister to my spirit. By your grace and healing power bring me to life. Complete the task that my earthly parents failed to do. I forgive my parents for not giving me the affection I needed, for not being there for me, for not affirming me, or holding me enough, and for not following God's commandment to nurture and awaken my spirit and bring me to life.

Lord, come and awaken my slumbering spirit. Resurrect it to life. Loose it from the grasp of the enemy. Help me accept your love and feel your touch. I bind my spirit to your Holy Spirit and to your love. Restore to me fourfold that which was taken from me in childhood and in life. Restore to me my innocence, my zest for life, my sensitivity and my ability to be intimate with you and others. Enable me to have hope, to use my creative abilities, to have spiritual inspiration when I am in your presence or reading your Word, to have an awareness of my spirit and the spirits of others, to exhibit vitality and strength of mind and to have the ability and the desire to experience the glory of sexual union with my spouse.

Lord, I confess to you and repent of my sins of resentment, anger and bitterness toward my dad and mom, for their failures and omissions. I ask you to loose me from the effects of those sins. Father God, forgive me for the many ways I have withdrawn from intimacy in my life. Also for the judgments and negative expectations I've held in my heart toward my dad and mom and others. I acknowledge this as sin and truly repent.

Lord, also forgive me for trying to win love and acceptance without the willingness or spiritual ability to hold my heart open to others. In the name of Jesus Christ, I tear down all the strongholds (habits, attitudes, values and beliefs) I have built to support my bitterness. Father, I take them all to the cross of Jesus and crucify them now and forever. Lord, I ask you to restore all that has been destroyed in my judgments against my dad and mom and others in my life. Lord, I also ask you to forgive my father and mother and to set them free.

Lord, I am willing to fully forgive my parents and others and loose them from my judgments. I accept your forgiveness for my sins, and I ask you to help me fully accept your forgiveness and love.

Lord, at this time I declare to you and to myself that I choose life, and I choose it more abundantly as your Word promises. I understand that abundant life is one filled with your peace, love, joy and prosperity; a life where my value is based on who I am in Jesus Christ and my hope is based on your grace and love which is never-ending. Lord, fill me with life and give me the strength of spirit to persist in risking to choose life. Enable me and encourage me to be vulnerable to those you sent to nurture me (body, mind, spirit and soul). Set me free from this slumber and empower me to bring life and joy to others as you intended.

In Jesus' name, Amen.

The Barrier of Evil Strongholds

Back in the first session of healing prayer, we introduced to clients the reality of evil forces that both perpetuate their pain and throw up barriers to their healing. In order to pray with power, your own understanding of these evil forces and how to overcome them must be clear. I'll confess, however, that my own learning about the reality and influence of the demonic in our world didn't really come until I began to actively minister in the Third World.

My first exposure came as a missionary doctor in the islands off the port of Inchon, South Korea. I had heard from others animism was the dominant religious belief there, and that people regularly consulted with witch doctors to find ways to appease the evil spirits that plagued them. During one of my clinics, a local witch came with a physical complaint. The exam proceeded very normally until in our conversation, I spoke the name of Jesus. The witch literally catapulted straight up like a jack-in-the-box and bolted out the door. I never saw her again.

This experience caught my attention, as you can imagine, so in the years ahead as I ministered in other parts of the developing world, and heard stories from my medical colleagues about their encounters with evil, I asked many questions. As it turned out, our Luke Society director in Ghana arranged for a conversation between Eleanor and me and a brother/sister duo who had been a wizard and witch, but had since committed their lives to Jesus Christ. They dramatically opened our eyes to both the reality and the methodology of evil at work.

Their mother and grandmother had both been witches, and passed on this spirit of evil to the two of them "through water, our bath water, when we were young," they told us. "But we liked it because it gave us power. We could start fights, or cause blow-outs and bad accidents. We could go other places and do these things, too (a practice known as astral travel)." But there was a high price to be paid for these powers. "We had to do terrible things to keep these powers," the woman shook her head. "I had to kill three of my ten children." Eleanor and I weren't sure we had heard correctly, and looked to the physician who was serving as our translator for confirmation. "It's true," he shook his head sadly. "Once she asked a witch doctor to put a curse on one of her enemies. He demanded the life of one of her children as payment, so at night she brought a small animal to be sacrificed, and within a few days after the witch doctor killed the animal, her child died. The other two children were sacrificed in a similar way to pay for other curses." Unbelievable. Quite honestly, because of my rational, Western upbringing, there was the fleeting temptation to dismiss such a horrific story as a tall tale. But I knew our physician/translator well. Trained in a first-rate medical school and having recently passed medical exams stringent enough to qualify him to practice in all parts of the United Kingdom, I knew he was bright, knowledgeable, and not given to superstition or silliness.

"What about Christians?" I asked the couple. "We couldn't harm them," they said. "It's like there is an invisible shield of light completely surrounding them." Their description made me think of an electromagnetic shield the evil couldn't penetrate.

As we first began to learn about these evil influences and saw more evidence, like the blood-stained porches of the witch doctors' houses in countries where we traveled, we assumed this activity must be driven by the superstitious bent of the Third World, and therefore must take place there exclusively. However, now that we are more aware, we've seen U.S. news reports of law enforcement officers finding evidence of blood sacrifices offered in isolated areas and social groups like Wiccans meeting on college campuses. Just because most of us in the West are unaware doesn't mean these evil influences aren't present and active.

There are four levels to demonic influence: temptation (which we all experience), oppression (which some experience more than others), infestation (the spirits actually enter our body but can never control us as Christians) and possession (in which the person no longer has a will of his own, but is totally controlled by the spirits.) Possession cannot occur to a person who has declared faith in Jesus Christ, but our own ignorance about evil influences or openness to them can allow evil to tempt, oppress or infest us as believers.

Where do these spirits come from, and how did they get a place of influence in the lives of ones who belong to Christ? There are four ways this can occur. The most common entry is through traumatic events in people's lives. These events cause wounding, and Satan latches onto these wounds and intensifies them, increasing anger, low self-image, feelings of inadequacy and anxiety, etc. (Does this mean that we should leave healing prayer and move into the exorcism business? No, because bringing these wounds to Jesus for healing does, in effect, "exorcise" the spirits of evil. It's as if there is no longer anything for evil to attach to, and they leave.)

Another portal can be through love for occultish things such as Ouija boards, or the Dungeons and Dragons game some play religiously. Tarot cards, witchcraft, fortune telling, psychic phenomena, séances—none of these are harmless games. They open the door to evil as do movies which glorify evil or Satanic activity. Habitual sin is another portal for evil spirits. Various addictions to drugs, alcohol, sex, pornography all fall into this category.

A fourth, and intensely dangerous portal, is through Satan worship and Satanic Ritual Abuse. We have not encountered any clients who were deeply into this kind of Satanic activity, but if we do, we're aware this person may need to be ministered to by others with particular gifting and expertise in this area.

As you've read, growing in this healing prayer ministry, we've had some personal experiences with spirits of evil with clients. These experiences are uncommon, but because we were prepared to expect their possible emergence, we were able to minister Christ's power and help.

I think now of the first client we dealt with who was being clearly influenced in a powerful way by Satan. John started playing the Dungeons and Dragon game as a lonely, withdrawn boy. Playing gave him a feeling of control and power; his parents assumed it was a harmless pastime. This influence showed itself during a Prayer for Inner Healing session with John. As he moved to prayer, he began to moan and wail. Eleanor, who was with him at the time, felt a moment of panic, but quickly was able to remember that we'd been taught this might happen, and it was nothing to fear. As John continued to wail, she stretched out her right hand toward him, and in the most authoritative voice she could muster commanded in Jesus' name that the spirit oppressing John leave him. She repeated the command until John calmed down. At the end of the session, John reported to us that he felt totally exhausted. We've since found that this is a common experience after someone has battled with an evil presence. However, in Jesus Christ, the battle is won, for God promises that "He that is in us is greater than he that is in the world" (I John 4:4).

It is essential to remember that Jesus gave authority over the spirits of evil to his disciples (Matthew 10:1). In his name we can take authority over the forces of evil and expect them to obey Christ's commands, given through us.

More commonly, the evil shows itself in the healing prayer session in the way it happened with Ruth. When she brought up the terrible memories of episodes of sexual assault from her father and tried to release them to the Lord, she froze. She whispered, "I just wanted a father so bad. It hurt so bad," and began clutching her chest and neck, her breathing becoming faster and more shallow. I wasn't sure if she was having a panic attack or if demonic involvement was manifesting itself, but Eleanor and I commanded any demons present to leave in the name of Jesus. We reminded them that Ruth belonged to Jesus and was protected by his blood. Then we asked God to come with his healing presence, and both began to pray quietly in the Spirit. After a time, Ruth breathed more deeply, and she became quiet and relaxed.

As she opened her eyes, she told us what had been happening in her while we prayed. "I had a deep pain in my heart. I couldn't breathe. My head and neck hurt with tension. It felt as if there was fire in my chest—a burning, a sharp pain—and then it began easing. I could breathe again. The hurting and tenseness in my heart disappeared, and I got a vision. A light was coming into a dark tunnel in me. It was as if the light was chasing the darkness away. Hands were pulling the tension apart—there was a loosening, loosening, loosening." She smiled. "You know I couldn't even say my father's name before." Then she spoke his name aloud over and over, and prayed a prayer of blessing on him to the Lord.

I have often thought about this experience and pictured it this way. It was as if Ruth's spirit was a dirigible bobbing just above the ground with multiple tethers keeping it from soaring as it was meant to. In prayer most of the tethers had been severed; her father was the last still in place. When God cut that rope during our last prayer session, she took off. Her whole life changed; she is now not only free and joyful, but she is enrolled in a nursing program, something she would never have imagined in her wounded state. She doesn't believe anything can stop her, now that she is deeply connected to God.

The Apostle Paul gives a very powerful teaching that has helped guide as well, as we encountered evil forces. It says this. "The weapons we fight with are not the weapons of the world. On the contrary, they have divine power to demolish strongholds. We demolish arguments and every pretension that sets itself up against the knowledge of God, and we take captive every thought to make it obedient to Christ" (2 Corinthians 10:4-5). The strongholds in our lives are areas on which Satan has a grip. Arguments, pretension and thoughts represent all the ways we insist on thinking or acting differently from God's truth. The following prayer, **Shattering Strongholds**, allows for a powerful commitment to bind all of our lives to Jesus.

Prayer Focus:

Prayer to Shatter Strongholds

CLIENT reads aloud in presence of PRAYER MINISTER:
In the name of Jesus Christ, I bind my body, soul and spirit to the will and purposes of God.
- *I bind myself to the truth of God.*
- *I bind myself to an awareness of the power of the blood of Christ working in my life every day.*

- *I bind my mind to the mind of Christ that I may have the thoughts, purposes and feelings of his heart in me.*
- *I bind my feet to the paths God has ordained me to walk, that my steps will be strong and steady.*
- *I bind myself to the work of the cross with all its mercy, truth, love, power, forgiveness and dying to self.*
- *In the name of Jesus Christ, I bind the strong man. I loose his hold on everything he has ever stolen from me.*
- *I rebuke his work and loose the power and effects of every deception, device, and influence he wants to bring against me.*

Lord, I repent of having wrong attitudes and thoughts.

- *I renounce them now and ask for forgiveness.*
- *I loose every old, wrong pattern of thinking, attitude, idea, belief, desire, habit and behavior that may still be working in me.*
- *I tear down, crush, smash and destroy every stronghold I have erected to protect them.*
- *I bind myself to the attitudes and patterns of Jesus Christ.*
- *I bind myself to the overcoming behavior and spiritual desires that line up with the fruit of the Holy Spirit.*

Father, I loose any stronghold in my life protecting wrong feelings I have against anyone.

- *Forgive me as I forgive those who have caused me grief, loss or pain.*
- *I loose any desire for retribution or vengeance.*
- *Help me bless those who have wronged me.*

In the name of Jesus, I loose the power and effects of any harsh or hard words (word curses) spoken about me, to me or by me.

- *I loose any strongholds connected with them.*
- *I loose all generational bondages and their strongholds from myself.*

Thank you, Jesus, that you have promised that whatever I bind or loose on earth will be bound or loosed in heaven (Matthew

16:19). *Amen* (Liberty S. Savarad, *Shattering Your Strongholds*, Bridge-Logos Publishers, North Brunswick, NJ, 1992).

Preparing for the Next Session:

Experiencing healing for inner wounds is an amazing journey! But it's just a part of the larger journey of a lifetime of growing intimacy with Jesus. We must help clients who have received this wonderful grace of healing "continue to live in him, rooted and built up in him, strengthened in the faith ... and overflowing with thankfulness" (Colossians 2:6, 7). We'll move next to directions for living, and continuing to grow in, a life of spiritual health and vitality.

Miscarriage Recovery

On her intake form, Sonja listed bitterness and unforgiveness as issues. However, instead of childhood wounds, the Spirit led us to talk about a miscarriage on Thanksgiving Day several years earlier. As the conversation began, her tears began, as well, and she grieved for the baby's death.

As the Lord touched her in prayer, she was able to release this unborn baby to his care, and later talked with her husband about the impact of the miscarriage on her, bringing them to a new closeness. The following Thanksgiving was a different experience—she reported enjoying it.

CHAPTER EIGHT

Staying Healthy

"You were taught, with regard to your former way of life, to put off your old self...to be made new in the attitude of your minds, and to put on the new self, created to be like God in true righteousness and holiness."

EPHESIANS 4:22-24

Here's a wonderful episode in the healing life of Jesus. Mark, in his gospel records, "Simon's mother-in-law was in bed with a fever, and they told Jesus about her. So he went to her, took her hand and helped her up. The fever left her and she began to wait on them" (Mark 1:30-31). As you can imagine, I like this story because it shows so clearly the compassionate, healing touch of Jesus at work in the life of one who was suffering. But even more powerful is this: the fever left her—healing, to God's glory—then, "she began to wait on them." Her healing freed her to go forward in a Jesus-focused, Jesus-pleasing service to him and to others.

That's our intention for those with whom we pray. Christ enters their lives through these times of prayers while they are broken and wounded, and we see him heal and restore. But when they leave these sessions, they should go, as Peter's mother-in-law did, equipped to continue in their healing and liberated to serve Christ and his people.

There is another side to consider, as well. We not only rejoice in clients' strength for service, but we also pay attention to their vulnerability if they do not continue in the healing they've received. I think this is the warning inherent in another of Jesus' stories, this one a parable. "When an evil spirit comes out of a man," Jesus began, "it goes through places seeking rest and does not find it. Then it says, 'I will return to the house I left.' When it arrives it finds the house swept clean and put in order. Then it goes and takes seven other spirits more wicked than itself, and they go in and live there. And the final condition of that man is worse than the first" (Luke 11:24-27). There are many ways this passage can be applied, but for us, I think it offers an important wisdom. Inner healing must be a beginning, not just an end. We need now to equip clients to continue to grow in Christ, becoming strengthened to be their own prayer ministers in the months and years ahead.

We are going to consider together three areas of equipping clients need to consider as we conclude our time together. They are these encouragements:

- Change what you can; release what you can't to God.
- Activate the defense system of God.
- Take on the mind of Christ.

Change What You Can; Release What You Can't

A number of years ago, a popular song made the rounds, called "If I Ruled the World." Even today the ambitious and somewhat naïve lyrics make me smile. "If I ruled the world, every day would be the first day of spring. Every heart would have a new song to sing, and we'd sing of the joy every morning would bring." Oh, my. I don't know about you, but every day for me isn't the first day of spring, and some mornings don't start out with anything close to joy—a little dizziness and a slight headache would be more like it. In reality, our experience is closer to the description provided in the book of Job. "Man is born to trouble as

After a year, Christy reported:

" It's just easier to give things to God each day. The prayers from conception to birth really lined things up for me—He was right there with me from the beginning."

"I no longer get angry when my daughter acts out. I teach my children responsibility. I'm at the gym three-four times a week and am eating more salad and fruit."

"I understand myself so much better, and know with confidence that God is right here. And that confidence is strengthening me— I'm planning to return to college."

surely as sparks fly upward" (Job 5:7). People—and especially people who follow Christ—who expect that somehow magically all troubles in their lives have disappeared once they've received God's healing for inner wounds—are setting themselves up to be knocked down.

"Life is difficult," author Scott Peck asserts as he began his bestselling book, *The Road Less Traveled.* But he goes on, "Most do not fully see this truth that life is difficult. Instead they moan more or less incessantly, noisily or subtly, about the enormity of their problems, their burdens, and their difficulties as if life were generally easy, as if life should be easy." And he concludes, "Life is a series of problems. Do we want to moan about them or solve them?" (*The Road Less Traveled*, M. Scott Peck, M.D, Simon & Schuster, New York, 1978, p. 15).

With the strengthening of Christ that comes from inner healing, our clients are now differently ready to accept Peck's problem-solving challenge. They know from personal experience that they are no longer alone, and that Christ is a daily, intimate friend who now shares the joys—and problems—of the journey with them bringing healing, grace, comfort, strength and power.

It is with this confidence we talk with clients about what's ahead, and often speak with them about what we call the "Change Triangle." It looks like this:

GOD

Me   Others

We're not solo entities; we live in the context of two other relationships: our relationship with God, and our relationship with others. When those horizontal relationships cause us trouble (and they will, as surely as "the sparks fly upward"), our temptation is to try to change the other person or people, so they become less troublesome and our lives get easier. When this approach works, we rejoice and give thanks! But when it doesn't, we're left stuck in a quandary. Our lives aren't happy with problem-people left unchanged, yet we've been unsuccessful in changing them. Are we then at the mercy of these problem-creators, doomed to live less than the abundant life God promised?

Not at all! God himself has chosen, out of his love and respect for us, to limit his capacity to force changes. When Jesus looked at the city—and the people—he came to save, he wept because though he longed to gather them to himself, he said, "You were not willing" (Luke 13:34). So, when others cause us problems, our peace is best served if, instead of trying to initiate horizontal solutions, we begin with the vertical—going to God, taking the person and the problem to God in prayer, asking first for his grace and help. Our clients will know because of how they've seen God respond to them already that he is fully ready and willing to do this! They know, too, that he can release them from the pain caused by problematic people who can't or won't change, because they've already experienced this release

After a year, Jane reported:

"The Four-Way Forgiveness Prayer got rid of my hurts. My faith is so much stronger now. I trust God with my life. I love to please him, and focus on doing the works of Christ. My husband sees a difference, and I'm more patient with my children. I no longer gossip, and my eyes are open to those in hurt."

"My relationship is so much closer to God. He speaks through his Word, answers my prayers, and has given me more faith."

"Now I'm a woman living for her purpose in God. We changed churches and have become very active, plus read the Bible and pray daily."

"And, I've lost 33 pounds!"

in their deepest selves. So, we coach clients that when going forward, others cause them grief or pain, they first respond by appropriating the Four-Way Forgiveness Prayer. They can forgive and seek forgiveness from God. They can bless and seek blessing from God. From this place of clarity and strength, they are then ready to hear from God what, if anything, he might want them to do about those who trouble them.

Another prayer that can equip clients for responding victoriously to challenging people or circumstances is the **Prayer to Be Set Free**. This powerful prayer was adapted from an original created by our prayer mentor, Francis MacNutt.

Lord Jesus, I realize that the sickness and evil I encounter is more than my humanity can bear. So cleanse me of any sadness, negativity or despair, or any lies of Satan that I may have picked up.

If I have been tempted to anger, impatience, lust, harshness, evil thoughts, vindictiveness, discouragement or lack of self-control, cleanse me of these temptations and replace them with love, joy, goodness, self-control and peace. If any evil spirits have attached themselves to me or oppressed me in any way, I command them to depart from me now, and go straight to Jesus Christ for him to deal with as he wills.

Come, Holy Spirit. Renew me, fill me anew with your power, your life and your joy. Strengthen me where I have felt weak and clothe me with your light. Fill me with life.

Lord Jesus, please send your holy angels to minister to me and my family—and to guard us from all sickness, harm and accidents.

I praise you now and forever, Father, Son and Holy Spirit. Amen.

Praying this prayer in the face of challenge puts control of our clients' lives squarely back in God's hands, exactly where we want them to be. Interestingly, once our lives are in God's control, they're also in our control, as well. We're one with Christ, so inviting his control in our lives leaves us safe, strong and equipped with all we need to meet whatever comes.

Activate the Defense System of God

Many tell us that one of the most helpful "side benefits" of the healing prayer experience is a new understanding of spiritual warfare—the reality of Satan as our enemy and the power of Christ to defeat him, and some ways to confront and overcome him. Going forward, this equipping can be the beginning of a life lived with freedom and confidence to stand against and overcome evil.

The Apostle Paul gave us excellent direction in how to go about preparing for such a life, when he told Christians at Ephesus to "Be strong in the Lord and in his mighty power. Put on the full armor of God so that you can take your stand against the devil's schemes" (Ephesians 6:10-11). Paul paints a picture of Christ's followers standing strong and sure against evil. No crouching fainthearted in a corner, hands over our heads, trying to hide from the devil. No! Equipped with the safety and protection of God's armor and the powerful weapon of his Word, we stand firm, ready to declare to the forces of evil that they have no place, no power, no dominion over us as children of God.

Our battle cry is this, "Submit yourselves to God, resist the Devil and he will flee!" (James 4:7). We submit ourselves to God by releasing our problems and pains to him, as we've just discussed, and taking on the mind of Christ, a discipline we'll discuss shortly. Between these two, we resist the Devil by looking to God and his defense system, not by resorting to some of the defenses we've crafted for ourselves over the years to protect from hurt—denial, withdrawal, anger, criticism, blaming and others. As clients have learned through these sessions, their connection to God is a powerful defense against the enemy of our souls.

We leave clients with a prayer that can have great power in protecting themselves and their families as well, from the Devil's harassment. We encourage them to pray it daily, standing now as a warrior against evil, not just for themselves, but for those they love. It's called the **Prayer of Family Protection**.

Lord Jesus, thank you for my family. I ask that you protect [name family members]

- *From sin*
- *From sickness*
- *From accidents of every kind and*
- *From the evil one.*

If we have been subjected to any curses, hexes or spells, I break them and declare them null and void in the name of Jesus Christ. I decommission any evil spirits sent against us, and I send those spirits to Jesus Christ to do with as he wills, according to his justice and wisdom. If there are any spirits not of Jesus Christ trying to harm or influence our family in any way, I command you to stop it immediately, depart and not come back.

After a year, Lisa reported:

"I see God clearer, and what he is doing, and my faith keeps getting stronger as I see him answering more and more prayers."
"I'm communicating so much better with others. Maybe it's because I'm much stronger and not swayed by others. But I'm also
no longer ashamed of things in my past; they don't pull on me. I
now have more concern for others, and more friends."

---

*Lord Jesus, I ask you to send your Holy Spirit to fill us today
with your life, your health and your guidance to show us what
you want us to do today. Help us become like you, Jesus, and fill
us with your love, your joy, your peace and your compassion.
Make us be more and more like you and empower all our prayers
to help your people.*

Thanks be to God. Amen.

Taking on the Mind of Christ

A number of times in our learning, we've walked with our client
Ruth, who moved through healing prayer from a place of deep
brokenness to clear expressions of joy and release. Now, has
healing taken place in her life? The answer is yes, absolutely! But
is she healed? The answer is, not yet. Though God has delivered
her from bondage to negative emotions that were attached to
her memories, the thought patterns generated by these hurtful
memories are still present in her brain. They need to be replaced
by learning to think—and then to function—in a God-pleasing
way, thinking the thoughts of the mind of Christ. Practically
speaking, how can this replacement take place?

Remember our early delving into the realm of brain science?
It teaches that new thought patterns can be formed by focused
mental concentration, something scientists call "self-induced

neuroplasticity." Clients can change deeply-embedded brain patterns by choosing new inputs and finding good ways to focus on those positive inputs.

To provide the input she needs, we turned Ruth to the Word of God. That's why each session includes some connection to the Word of God, and often verses to take home and meditate on. We told her, "Read these verses until you find one that speaks to you. Take that verse and pray it back to God. Write it out, put it on your bathroom mirror or another place where you see it frequently. Be sure to carry it with you during the day. Concentrate on it. Memorize it. Ask God how it can become real in your life."

Is an assignment like this unrealistic for clients busy with work and family? It depends on priorities. President Obama's mother got him up at 5 a.m. every morning to do his homework—and then made breakfast and went to work herself. His education was her priority, so she found a way to make it happen. I often tell clients, "If I could promise you a million dollars if you got up at 5 a.m. to meditate on these verses every day for a year, would you commit to it?" Most smile and nod. "Well," I reply, "I don't have a million dollars to offer, but with your commitment and God's help you will experience the abundant life Jesus promised—worth much more than a million dollars!"

Your clients may have been dedicated Christian believers for years, yet still see sin patterns in their lives. They might say, "This is me. I'm just wired this way." How wrong! Sinful habits aren't permanent in the life of those in Christ. The four Steps of Meditation in Chapter 5 applied to highly targeted Scriptures will enable them to conquer old patterns of thinking, acting and reacting. In the process Satan's strongholds are destroyed in their lives. We ask clients to identify areas they consider particularly and habitually troublesome (for example, anger), and encourage them to find a Scripture that specifically speaks to this area (for example, Ephesians 4:26, "In your anger do not sin. Do not let the sun do down while you are still angry"). We've already included an introduction to Scripture meditation and the value of using God's Word in our prayers in Chapters 5 and 6. Listed there are some key verses we use in early weeks of prayer sessions. Additional **Scriptures for Meditation** are found in the Appendix. While this is not an exhaustive list, it does provide ready access to a variety of categories. A targeted focus like this on God's Word will help clients create new life patterns.

Besides this emphasis on the Scripture, we encourage four other practices.

1. *Maintain fellowship with other believers.* Depression isolates us (Satan wants us isolated); anxiety causes us to focus on ourselves. Close relationships with trusted Christian friends can counteract both.

2. *Maintain your walk with God.* Practice the presence of God moment-by-moment in your life. Practice submission to God, so that he and nothing or no one else is on the throne of your life. "Draw near to God, and he will draw near to you" James 4:8.

3. *Live your life with a plan.* No one starts a business without a clear plan; how much more then, should we plan for how we'll feed our spirits through the Word, prayer and fellowship, and how we'll extend ourselves to others through service. If we aim at nothing, we'll hit it; continued growth requires that we plan for it.

However, plans also need flexibility. One of my early business mentors wisely advised me, "No company can succeed without goals, but the company that does the best is the one that doesn't always follow them." In other words, stay flexible. If God changes directions, change with him! Paul did this. He had plans for the ministry, but God altered these plans in a dream, changing the geographical focus of his ministry (Acts 16:6-10). We'd be wise to do the same.

4. *Guard your heart and mind.* All believers need to be alert to evil. However, our clients need to give special attention to inner pulls back into the negative thoughts and emotions that bound them for so long. They have come to know themselves

After a year, John reported:

"The prayers enabled me to put negative thoughts out of my
mind. I was previously worried about aging. I've let it go."
"Now I have a sense of purpose that makes me expectant, looking
forward to things—and everything is fun."

well, and have an understanding of the signs of depression and
anxiety. They are equipped to guard their minds. So, I challenge
them to visualize a very large, red STOP! sign. Every time their
thoughts start linking to negative emotions, that STOP! sign
comes out. Next, a quick shift to the positive should happen.
GO! In a new direction. Interrupting negative thoughts in their
early stages, and replacing them with positives is what it means
to "take captive every thought to make it obedient to Christ" (II
Corinthians 10:5). We never fight negative emotions; we replace
them. As we do, the way we think is transformed, and new life
becomes our daily habit.

Beyond Release to Soaring

The intention of healing prayer isn't just to *take away* wounds;
it's to *add to* our lives an experience of intimacy with God, others
and ourselves. As clients confess their sins, unload their hurts
and are healed of negative emotions, a new relationship with
God emerges. They begin living intentionally in the presence of
God, asking him daily, "What way do you want me to go? What
thinking do you want me to have?" The experiential presence of
God in their lives flows from them and touches others. The old
is gone; the new has come.

No Longer a Doormat

Sally was a talented teenager and National Honor Society member, and pretty enough for a teen glamour magazine. But her life story was anything but beautiful. Her parents gave her up because of their drug and alcohol addictions, so multiple foster homes and social abuse had been part of her life by age 14.

In one manifestation of her pain, she struggled with a "telephone" boyfriend who constantly threatened to "break up" with her. His threats resulted in day-long crying fits.

After healing prayer, her caretaker told us that when Sally came home, she was whistling. "Something good happen?" the caretaker asked. "I finally got my healing," Sally smiled. Ready evidence? The next time her boyfriend threatened to end their relationship, she said, "Then it's probably best we break up."

CHAPTER NINE

A Closing Note to Prayer Ministers: What to Do When You Don't Know What to Do

"My God will meet all your needs according to his riches in Christ Jesus."

PHILIPPIANS 4:19

A lady who has been a client for the past several months told us she never knew anyone could have the peace she has experienced since she has been coming to these prayer sessions. The truth is, God wants us all to have this deep, inner peace, this well-being or *shalom* in this life, not just in heaven. It comes from knowing God's love, forgiveness and power that releases us from the garbage we've carried. His work in our lives allows us to soar on wings like eagles (Isaiah 40:31).

As you seek to help others soar, there may be days when you feel stopped, stumped, overwhelmed. We have felt all of these. In order to keep on in this ministry of *innercession*, we've found four "updrafts" that have helped us continue in helping others to find release and intimacy with Christ.

Begin with Your Own Healing

You need to be a clear pipeline for God's love and healing. That means no harboring of known sin, no festering wound or anger, no secret you've been hiding from God. Bring these things to God. Use the prayers we've been studying as prayers for yourself first.

Perhaps begin with the Submission Prayer. Then pray the Four-way Forgiveness Prayer for every person you feel negative toward. Pray each part from your heart. Then spend some minutes of quiet, stilling your brain, allowing God to heal the deep hurts, one at a time. Feel the hurt and ask him to take it from you. Wait for him and listen carefully, with expectancy.

Pray any of the other prayers you may need for anyone who has wounded you, or for sinful behaviors you may have gotten into. Pray for a change of attitude; pray to totally submit to the Lord—see James 4:7-8. Learn to fight the battle against Satan. Get yourself connected to God through prayer, Bible study, music, or other activities that help you, until you feel you are an open vessel, able to be used by God to help others.

We've come to believe that the secret is to keep at it and be seeking a relationship with Christ who loves you more than anybody else ever could. That's where your own peace as a Prayer Minister comes from. (A book that helped Eleanor particularly in her search for a deeper experience of Christ was *Passion for Jesus* by Mike Bickle.)

Living life this way has made us much more accountable to God. We can't overlook habitually wrong patterns; we can't stay in self-pity or blame. We're determined to be a clear pipeline for God's healing. As we tend to our own spiritual experience, we've found that *Released to Soar* can be a daily reality for us, just as it is for our healed clients.

Trust God's Promises to Help

The Scripture verses that gave Eleanor courage to get started praying alone with clients are found in the New Living Translation of Isaiah 50:4 and 7: "The Sovereign Lord has given me his words of wisdom, so that I know what to say to all these weary ones. Morning by morning he awakens me and opens my understanding to his will. Because the Sovereign Lord helps me, I will not be dismayed. Therefore, I have set my face like a stone, determined to do his will. And I know that I will triumph." She clung to these Scriptures every morning before leaving for the prayer room, and God kept—and continues to keep—his promises.

God promises in Matthew 7:11: "If you, then, though you are evil, know how to give good gifts to your children, how much more will your Father in heaven give good gifts to those who ask him!" God wants to give healing—and all good gifts—to our clients, and he's chosen us as his partners in this wonderful work. Therefore we can relax and expect his help.

We hope you will find many of the verses in this book useful. God gave the Scriptures we've supplied for meditation to Eleanor as we began the ministry. There are so many others in the Bible that would be equally helpful, of course, and we encourage you to find verses on your own, asking God to help you, especially those that directly address your areas of concern.

Listen for Discernment

Some people have the gift of discernment described in I Corinthians 12. Actually, we don't believe we have this gift. However, God helps us help others anyway. Here's how it works. We pray daily for the discernment we need to be useful in God's purposes. Also, we ask again as we begin with each client in the session. Because we trust that God wants each client to be freed of whatever Satan is using to bind them, we believe God will work through our minds (or any other way he chooses) to accomplish this healing.

As Eleanor types up the session notes after being with a client, she continues to pray for the Spirit's guidance. Often we will get strong ideas for that client and make note of these thoughts. When we review the notes before the next session, we ask again for God's guidance to go in the direction he sets for that day. Time and time again, we see him heal the person.

We're clear the healing didn't come from us, but there is nothing impossible for God to do. We marvel and thank him each time a client describes experiences after inner healing. Often it is his deep inner peace. They describe feeling lighter; they have a look of calm and contentment about them. How gratified— and full of praise—we feel when we hear in one-year-follow-up stories of the marvelous ways God has gone on to bless clients. God promises to help us minister, and he is faithful.

Don't Try to Do God's Job

A sixteen-year-old came today who recently found out that she is pregnant. Her story is like that of so many: anger at a bio- logical dad who never claimed her, has broken every promise he ever made and tells her she is good for nothing. Satan's lies have come hurling at her through this man.

God began his redeeming work in her life today, reclaiming her life from Satan by letting her know he loves her and has forgiven her. Here's the interesting part. When we finished, she said she now believed God's protection would be with her and her unborn baby. However, *we never directly prayed for these things.*

We simply prayed the Four-way Forgiveness prayer for her biological father. Then we just had time for a brief Conception to Birth Prayer, in which Eleanor prayed for the young woman during her prenatal period. The client, however, understood Eleanor's prayer to be directed toward the baby inside her, and she told us of the peace and strength she felt when she considered God caring for her unborn child in this way.

God used the prayer in the way he knew she needed it most. We didn't have to know any of this. You see, God uses us in spite of ourselves. This healing is from him, not from us. We don't have to know everything in order to help others; we just have to be willing.

As you share this journey with wounded ones who seek Christ's healing touch, you become his voice, his hands, his representative in bringing light and life to those he loves. You are a partner with Christ in his healing. We rejoice with you at the privilege of this ministry, and we pray for you the prayer Paul penned for his co-ministers at Ephesus.

"I pray that out of his glorious riches he may strengthen you with power through his Spirit in your inner being, so that Christ may dwell in your hearts through faith. And I pray that you, being rooted and established in love, may have the power, together with all the saints, to grasp how wide and long and high and deep is the love of Christ, and to know this love that surpasses knowledge—that you may be filled to the measure of all the fullness of God.

Now to him who is able to do immeasurably more than all we ask or imagine, according to his power that is at work within us, to him be glory in the church and in Christ Jesus throughout all generations, forever and ever!

Amen, and Shalom.

Peter and Eleanor

Prayer Intake Form

Name:_____ Date:_____

Address: _____

Phone: Home _____ Business _____ Cell _____

Fax: _____ E-mail: _____ Date of Birth _____

Occupation: _____ Employment: _____ Marital Status: _____

Children: (names, ages) _____

_____

Referred by: _____ Church: _____

In your own words, what are the reasons you are coming for healing prayer?

a) _____

b) _____

Health History

Have you had any major medical, surgical or accident experience? If so, please describe: _____

_____

Are you under the care of a physician, psychiatrist, or counselor/ therapist? If so, please describe: _____

_____

3) What medications are you presently taking? _____

_____

4) How do you spend your leisure time? _____

Spiritual History

1) Briefly describe your religious background as a child: _____

_____

_____

2) Are you a Christian? _____ Yes _____ No _____ Uncertain

3) When did you become a Christian? _____

4) Church involvement (Circle the appropriate number):

	1	2	3	4	5
	very active				detached

4) Bible reading:

	1	2	3	4	5
	daily		monthly		infrequently

5) Prayer:

	1	2	3	4	5
	daily		monthly		infrequently

6) Occult (Please circle items): Ouija board, seances, horoscopes, tarot cards, psychic power, witchcraft, or other _____

7) Was anyone in your ancestry involved in the occult, New Age, Satanism, cults, spiritism, Masonic, Eastern Star, etc.?

If so, describe: _____

_____

8) Have you ever been *socially or sexually* involved with one who has been involved in any of the above?

If so, describe: _____

Family Background

1) Describe the atmosphere in your family of origin: _____

_____

_____

2) Describe your relationship with your father as a child and growing up: _____

_____

_____

3) Describe your relationship with your mother as a child and growing up: _____

_____

4) Are your parents still living? _____

Are your parents living together?_____

5) Pregnancy (when your mother was pregnant with you) difficult or easy? _____

6) Siblings: Brothers _____ Sisters _____ Your birth order: _____

7) Describe your relationship with your siblings past and present:

_____

_____

Emotional History

Place a check mark in the blank for statements which are true.

1) _____ I don't remember being physically loved as a child (hugs, being held, etc.)

2) _____ My parents were divorced when I was _____ years old.

3) _____ I had no father growing up—death / divorce / preoccupation. (circle one)

4) _____ One of my parents committed suicide when I was _____ years old.

5) _____ I was adopted.

6) _____ I have a handicap that brought ridicule from peers.

7) _____ Do you have a recurrent memory of a past hurt?

8) _____ I was greatly embarrassed as a child or young adult.

9) _____ I had an alcoholic/drug abusing parent.

10) _____ I have had one or more abortions.

11) _____ I have had one or more miscarriages.

12) _____ I have a physical illness that has no known cause.

13) _____ I can see a pattern of hurtful events beginning in early childhood and building on one another.

14) _____ I dislike myself.

15) _____(Circle and complete) I'm controlled by habits of smoking, alcohol, pornography, sexual thoughts and have a fantasy world into which I escape. Other _____

16) _____ How much alcohol do you consume in a week? _____

17) _____ I use cocaine, marijuana or other drugs.

18) _____ I have unreasonable fears.

19) _____ I have overwhelming feelings of guilt.

20) _____ There are people I can't forgive.

21) _____ I find it difficult admitting to mistakes and blame others for what goes wrong in my life.

22) _____ I have significant feelings of anger inside.

23) _____ I'm often critical in my remarks or thoughts of others.

24) _____ I suffer from recurrent troubling dreams or nightmares.

25) _____I feel guilty when I'm not doing something "productive."

26) _____ I constantly strive for the approval of others.

27) _____ I suffer from physical and mental exhaustion wrestling with inner problems.

28) _____ I go on compulsive binges of overeating, undereating, or drinking.

29) _____ I have had a break with reality.

30) _____ I have had hallucinations or heard voices in my head.

31) _____ I have sometimes found myself in places and do not remember how I got there.

32) _____ I have had times when I was not my usual self and I felt so good or so hyper that other people thought I was not my normal self.

33) _____ I have sometimes cut myself destructively.

34) _____ I have struggled with thoughts of suicide.

35) _____ I have a current plan for suicide.

Spiritual Oppression

1) _____ Inner perception of a separate personality, name or voice that prompts undesirable thoughts or behaviors.

2) _____ Fearful, repetitive night visitations by a fearful presence.

3) _____ Inability to focus on or retain Biblical truth.

4) _____ Difficulty participating in prayer.

5) _____ Extreme nervousness or negative reactions at the mention of the name of Jesus.

6) _____ Preoccupation with thoughts of death, despair and hopelessness.

Please list other factors which lead you to believe that you are experiencing spiritual oppression:

_____

_____

_____

_____

Checklist of Identifying Difficulties:

*Please **rate each item** on a **scale of 1 to 5** with **1 being the lowest and 5 being the most severe.***

_____ Depression

_____ Stress

_____ Physical Abuse

_____ Marital Problem

_____ Panic Attacks

_____ Sexual Abuse

_____ Drug Addiction

_____ Low Self-Esteem

_____ Verbal/Emotional Abuse

_____ Smoking Addiction

_____ Insomnia

_____ Guilt

_____ Eating Disorder

_____ Relationships

_____ Occult Oppression

_____ Workaholism

_____ Sexual Identity Problem

_____ Unforgiveness / Bitterness

_____ Anxiety/Fear

_____ Loneliness

_____ Suicidal Thoughts

_____ Anger

_____ Rejection

_____ Chronic Illness

_____ Pornography

_____Grief/Loss

Occult Practices

(EPHESIANS 4:27, 6:10-18, I PETER 5:8-9)

Circle each one in which you have participated, even just for fun or out of curiosity.

Fortune Tellers/Soothsayers

(See Deuteronomy 18:9-16; Daniel 2:26-28, Isaiah 2:6, 47:10-15, Micah 5:12, Acts 16:16.)

1. Have you ever had your fortune told by tea leaves, palm reading, crystal ball, fortune teller, etc.?

2. Have you ever read or followed horoscopes, or had a chart made for you to predict your future?

3. Have you ever read any other types of birth signs?

4. Have you ever been hypnotized, practiced self-hypnosis, yoga with a mantra or transcendental meditation? (In Biblical days, hypnotism was spoken of as 'casting a spell' and a hypnotist was called a 'charmer.')

5. Have you ever been involved in charming or enchanting or other attempts to use spirit power?

Necromancy (communication with the dead), Spiritualism

(See I Samuel 28:7-11, II Kings 21:6, Isaiah 8:19-22, Leviticus 19:31, 20:6.)

6. Have you ever attended a séance or spiritualist meeting?

7. Do you believe in reincarnation or have you had a

reincarnation reading?

8. Have you ever played with a Ouija board, crystal ball, Dungeons & Dragons or other occult games?

9. Have you ever had a Tarot card reading or practiced cartonomacy (using playing cards for fortune telling or other magical purposes)?

10. Have you ever played games of an occult nature, using ESP, telepathy, hypnotism, etc.?

11. Have you ever consulted a medium, spiritualist or numerologist, or acted as a medium or practiced channeling?

12. Have you seen and/or communicated with apparitions that are not of God?

13. Have you ever sought healing through magic spells or charms, or through Christian Science or spiritualists? Have you ever sought psychic healing or had psychic surgery?

14. Have you ever practiced table lifting, levitation of objects, pendulum swinging, lifting of bodies, automatic writing, astral travel or soul-travel?

15. Have you ever used a charm or amulet of any kind for protection or 'good luck?' Are you superstitious?

16. Have you ever participated in chain letters?

17. To your knowledge have you ever practiced any other kinds of black arts?

Occult Books, 'Contact' Objects and Other Media

(See Deuteronomy 5:8-10, 7:4-6 and 25-26, I Kings 14:7-11, II Kings 23:1-25, Psalm 97: 7, Isaiah 42:17, Acts 19:19-20.)

18. Have you read or possessed books on astrology, interpretation of dreams, augury or interpretation of omens, cults or other religious groups which deviate from Scriptural Christian doctrine such as Christian Science, Unity, Scientology or Science of Mind?

19. Have you read or possessed books on witchcraft, fortune telling, magic, ESP, psychic phenomena or possession?

20. Do you have anything in your home that was given to you by someone in the occult or anything in your home of an occult nature?

21. Have you followed the writings of Edgar Cayce, Jean Dixon, Shirley MacLaine, L. Ron Hubbard, (Church of Scientology) or any other New Age author?

22. Do you find yourself interested in demonic types of movies such as *The Exorcist, Rosemary's Baby* or *The Omen*? Are you drawn to horror shows or scary movies such as *Friday the 13th*? Are you fascinated with evil or the occult?

23. Have you ever listened to hard or acid rock music with a satanic influence or music with a New Age influence?

24. Have you ever visited or worshipped in a shrine or temple of a non-Judeo/Christian religion? Do you possess any books, articles or statues from any of these religions?

Sorcery or Magic

(See II Kings 17:17, 21:6, Isaiah 47:9, Malachi 3:5, Acts 8:11, 13:4-12, Revelation 18:23, 21:8.)

25. Have you ever practiced sorcery or magic?

26. Have you ever practiced mind control over any person or animal, cast a magic spell or sought a psychic experience? Have you ever contacted a psychic in person or through a psychic hotline?

Sins of the Flesh, Sins of the Eyes

(See Matthew 5:28, Romans 6:12-14, 7:7-25, 8:13-14; I Corinthians 6:13 and 18-20, 9:26-27, Galatians 5:16-21, I Thessalonians 4:3-8, James 1:14-15, I Peter 2:11, I John 2:16.)

27. Have you ever used LSD, marijuana, cocaine, crack cocaine or any mind-expanding or mind-altering drugs? Have you ever abused prescription drugs? Have you ever viewed abstract art while under hallucinogenic stimulus?

28. Do you have a problem with alcohol?

29. Have you ever exposed yourself to pornography in magazines, Playboy pictures, TV or stage shows, books, topless bars or X-rated movies?

30. Have you ever had a problem with habitual masturbation?

31. Have you seen shows about sexual deviation, homosexuality or lesbianism?

32. Have you been involved in sexual deviation, homosexuality or lesbianism?

33. Have you been involved in group sex or bestiality?

34. Have you ever had sexual relations with a person who was not your legal spouse? If possible, recall them by name (first name or initial is sufficient).

35. Have you had an abortion? Have you fathered a child who was aborted?

36. Have you been involved in abortion in any way (viewed, witnessed one, assisted in one, performed one, encouraged a friend to have one, had a botched abortion, etc.)?

Devil Worship

(See II Chronicles 11:15, Psalm 106:37, I Corinthians 10:20-22, Revelation 9:20-21, 13:4.)

37. Have you ever made a pact with Satan or been involved in or witnessed Satan worship or black magic?

38. Have you ever worn, owned or had in your home the symbol of the ankh (a cross with a ring top that is used in satanic rites)?

39. Have you ever celebrated or witnessed a black mass?

40. Have you ever made a blood subscription or pact?

Witchcraft

(See Galatians 5:19-20, I Samuel 15:23, 28:7, II Kings 9:22; 23:24, I Chronicles 10:13, Isaiah 8:19, 19:3, 29:4; Micah 5:12.)

41. Have you ever attended witchcraft or voodoo activities?

42. Have you ever been involved in Freemasonry, Eastern Star or Rainbow Girls?

43. Have you ever wished someone else were dead or wished you were dead?

44. Have you ever planned or attempted to take your own life?

45. Have you ever planned or attempted to take someone else's life?

Generational Influences

(See Exodus 34:6-7, Numbers 14:17-19, Deuteronomy 5:8-10, Joshua 22:16-29, Psalm 33:11, Jeremiah 11:10-13, Acts 2:38-39.)

46. Have you or other family members had problems with drugs or alcohol?

47. Do you know of any relatives or ancestors who have been into witchcraft, pagan relations, fortune telling or strong superstitions, or used magic spells or potions?

48. Has anyone in your family been involved in Freemasonry, Eastern Star or Rainbow Girls?

Preparation of Family Tree

A family tree is used to diagram family history so you can see, at a glance, where problems are in each generation. Begin at the bottom of the family tree; fill in your name and your spouse's name, and any problems you have (if divorced, insert your previous spouse's name, too.) Do the same with your children, your parents and your brothers and sisters. Continue in this way up the family tree, as far as you can remember, indicating any patterns or problem areas in your family line. Some problems come down vertically, as from grandfather to father, some horizontally, from aunt to aunt, or cousin to cousin. Some of the problems are obvious, others are known only to God. Do not worry about what you do not know. Jesus will reveal what you need to know, and what he reveals he will bring into healing.

Great traumas may be healed through generational healing prayer without your knowing their exact cause. However, if you find that your family's problems are not completely resolved after one Holy Communion or healing prayer session, continue to intercede for them. In some cases, it may be necessary for prayer for the Healing of Generations to be repeated several times for family bloodlines. The following instructions provide some ideas to help prepare your family tree.

To construct your family tree, go back at least four generations, even if you do not know all names. If possible, check with parents, grandparents and other relatives to get more details or clearer information. Simply write on the family tree every issue that you would like to bring to the Lord. If you were adopted, you may have only a minimal amount of information regarding your biological family. In that case, include whatever information you have as to your biological family, as well as any pertaining to your adopted family. If you were adopted and are unaware of your biological family, simply include all the information pertaining to your adopted family.

Once you have finished constructing the family tree, look at the patterns in the family bloodlines. Below are some of the common areas of generational bondage that may help you form a more complete picture of your family tree. Remember to ask the Holy Spirit to reveal the truth. He may give you an area that is not listed below, but it is essential to put down all areas revealed to you in order to break the patterns of generational sin.

Unusual and Violent Deaths or Severe Trauma

Identify, by name, the people in your family who:
- Committed or attempted suicide.
- Were murdered or died in tragic ways such as accidents or wars.
- Committed an abortion or participated in/sponsored an abortion.
- Suffered repeated miscarriages.
- Died in a mental institution, nursing home, or prison (especially those who felt lonely, unloved and/or abandoned).
- Were not given a Christian burial (including committal services) or were unmourned.
- Suffered severe trauma, with evidence of effects passed on through the family (e.g., drowning, resulting in fear of water in other members, especially descendants).

Evidence of Occult or Demonic Activity

- Superstitions.
- Involved in the occult (e.g., witchcraft, astrology, spiritualism or divination).
- Opening one's self to powers in the spiritual realm, such as predicting the future.
- Made a blood covenant with Satan or was involved in satanic worship.
- Involved with a witch or other persons involved in the occult.

Habitual Patterns of Sin

Sexual sins:

- Adultery/fornication
- Prostitution
- Incest
- Pornography
- Lust
- Sexual promiscuity
- Sexual perversions

Be sure to list all sexual partners and/or any soul-ties you have with another. Even if it was not sexual you may be tied spiritually, emotionally, or mentally. If you are conjoined to another, you must be cut free from this relationship. Remember that Jesus does not separate us from a person when we have been tied to him or her in ways that are holy and within God's will. He only sets us free from the unholy or destructive part of the relationship. This is an especially important step when you are married or planning to marry.

Other habitual sins:

- Violence
- Abuse (physical, mental, emotional or spiritual)
- Racial prejudice
- Anger
- Religious prejudice
- Murder
- Pride
- Greed
- Materialism
- Hatred
- Unforgiveness
- Addictions (alcoholism, nicotine, drugs, food, etc.)
- Selfishness
- Judgments

Destructive or Abnormal Patterns of Relationships

- Abuse (emotional, mental, physical or spiritual)
- Hostility
- Control
- Manipulation
- Domination
- Revenge
- Unforgiveness
- Bitterness
- Anger

Diseases and/or Predispositions to Illness

- Arthritis
- Cancer
- Diabetes
- Depression/mood disorder
- Fibromyalgia
- Headaches
- Heart trouble
- High blood pressure
- Respiratory trouble
- Skin problems
- Ulcers

Historical Family Connections

- Involvement with events of great sin, evil or trauma (e.g., massacres, plagues, slavery, conquests, etc.).
- Ethnic origin issues, negative traits, cultural evils, oppression, or curses.

Religious History

- List all non-Judeo/Christian religions in the family or ancestral history (e.g., Islam, Buddhism, Native American).

In Utero Wounding

- Child conceived in lust or rape
- Illegitimacy
- Parent considering adoption or abandonment
- Fears/anxiety (e.g., mother had difficulty carrying child to term)
- Attempted/failed abortion
- Loss of father
- Life-threatening illness of the mother
- Life-threatening illness of the baby
- Mother had miscarriage(s) or abortion(s) before you were conceived
- Parent(s) wanted a child of the other sex

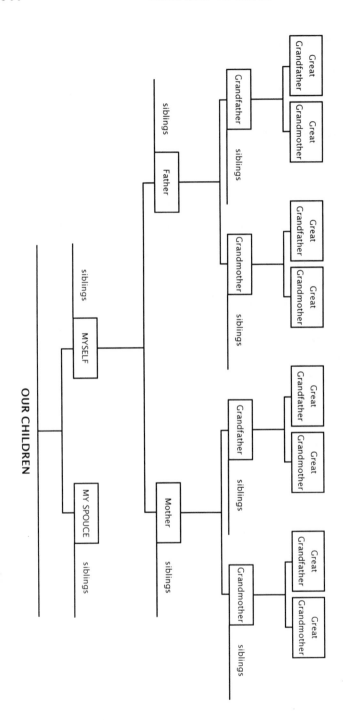

Family Tree

I. Prayer for the Healing of Generational Predispositions

Dear Lord, if there is any predisposition to _____
(alcoholism, lust, etc.) that has come down to me from my
parents, grandparents, etc. I ask you through your power to set
me free. Send your Holy Spirit, and by the power of your Holy
Spirit, and by the sword of your Spirit cut me free from any
predisposition to (repeat) _____.

Lord Jesus, in the place of weakness fill me with the power
of your Holy Spirit and fill me with your Spirit of (self-control,
confidence, courage, fortitude, or whatever fruit of the Spirit
counteracts this weakness I have). Thank you, Lord, for healing
me and my descendants. In your precious name I pray. Amen

II. Prayer of Command for the Healing of Spiritual Influences

In the name of Jesus Christ, I command you, spirit, to loose your
influence and hold upon me (this person). I command you to go
to Jesus Christ, our Lord and Savior, that he might deal with you
as he sees fit in his justice and mercy. You have intruded in my
(this person's) life long enough. Now go!

III. Prayer of Thanks for Generational Blessings

Dear Father, I thank you and praise your Holy Name for the
blessings of _____
(list them all) that have been passed down to me through my
family. I thank you for the faithfulness of those in my ancestry
who were godly, and I thank you that in any family, there are not
only inherited sins for which we should seek forgiveness, but
there are also some inherited blessings for which we can praise
you. Thank you, Lord. Amen

IV. Prayer for Cutting Generational Bondage

Heavenly Father, I come before you, in the blessed name of Jesus and in the power of the Holy Spirit. I thank you for sending Jesus by whose holy blood and precious sacrifice I and my loved ones can be set free from the brokenness, woundedness, sinful attitudes and negative patterns of my (our) ancestry. I thank you, Father, that you have called me to be free from all bondage in the name of Jesus, and I praise you that, in Christ, I shall be set free.

And now, Lord Jesus, gently reveal to me in the power of the Holy Spirit those ways in which I may be living out inherited sin patterns. All of these sin patterns, known and unknown to me, in my life and in the lives of my ancestors (in my spouse's life, in his/her ancestors, and in our offspring)—I acknowledge them all before you, Father. I confess to you the evil inclinations, compulsions and bad habits that have influenced us. I ask you to forgive me and all of my ancestors (my spouse and his/her ancestors and our offspring) for all these sins. In the name of Jesus and by his holy blood, set us free in you forever, Holy Father. Empty our souls of sin, and fill them with the holiness of Jesus.

I claim the Lord Jesus Christ as my true inheritance, and I thank you, Father, for the most wonderful gift of your Holy Son. I bless you, Jesus, that you have come to show me my true roots, which are within the very heart of God the Father. I praise you, Holy Trinity. Those whom the Son sets free are free indeed. Alleluia! Amen.

Submission Prayer

Jesus, I choose to be open and submitted to you today. I can and do trust you to be my protector, my shield and the revealer of my hurts.

Only you know what lies in the darkness, the deepest secrets inside of me. I ask that you reveal the deep and hidden things to me and my prayer minister. Search me, show us the hurts you want to heal today. I trust you not to give me more than I can handle.

I give you permission to dig deep for the roots of any hidden memories that are affecting my life. Take the keys to my heart and unlock the doors. Bypass any denial or deception that may be blocking my memory, anything that is still hindering me from receiving my healing.

Jesus, I ask you bring to the surface those things you wish to heal. I ask that you be with me as I re-experience any past hurt, pain, unmet need or unresolved issues in my life. I want to be set free by the power of the cross and the blood of Jesus.

In the name of Jesus I pray. Amen!

Intercessory Prayer for Clients

See footnote on page 49.

Additional Scriptures for Meditative Prayer

Distress

Isaiah 63:9 – In all their distress he too was distressed, and the angel of his presence saved them. In his love and mercy he redeemed them; he lifted them up and carried them all the days of old *(through all the years-NLT).*

Philippians 1:27-29 – That you stand firm in one spirit... without being frightened in any way by those who oppose you... For it has been granted to you on behalf of Christ not only to believe on him but also to suffer for him.

Psalm 103:3-5 – He forgives all my sins and heals all my diseases; he redeems my life from the pit and crowns me with love and compassion. He satisfies my desires with good things, so that my youth is renewed like the eagle's.

Isaiah 53:3-5 – He was despised and rejected...a man of sorrows, acquainted with bitterest grief. We turned our backs on him and looked the other way when he went by. He was despised, and we did not care. Yet it was our weaknesses he carried; it was our sorrows that weighed him down. And we thought his troubles were a punishment from God for his own sins! But he was wounded and crushed for our sins. He was beaten that we might have peace. He was whipped, and we were healed! (NLT)

Psalm 42:5 – Why are you downcast, O my soul? Why so disturbed within me? Put your hope in God, for I will yet praise him, my Savior and my God.

Matthew 11:28 – Come to me, all you who are weary and burdened, and I will give you rest.

Anxiety, Fear

Zephaniah 3:17 – For the Lord your God has arrived to live among you. He is a mighty savior. He will rejoice over you with great gladness. With his love, he will calm all your fears. He will exult over you by singing a happy song. (NLT)

Psalm 34:4 - I sought the Lord, and he answered me; he delivered me from my fears.

Psalm 34:7 - The angel of the Lord encamps around those who fear him, and he delivers them.

Psalm 56:3-4 - When I am afraid, I will trust in you...What can mortal man do to me?

Philippians 3:14-20 - Forgetting what is behind and straining toward what is ahead, I press on toward the goal to win the prize for which God has called me heavenward in Christ Jesus... But our citizenship is in heaven.

Philippians 4:6-7 - Don't worry about anything, instead, pray about everything. Tell God what you need, and thank him for all he has done. If you do this, you will experience God's peace, which is far more wonderful than the human mind can understand. His peace will guard your hearts and minds as you live in Christ Jesus.

Philippians 4:12-13 - I have learned the secret of being content in any and every situation... I can do everything through him who gives me strength.

I Peter 5:7-9 - Give all your worries and cares to God, for he cares about what happens to you. Be careful! Watch for attacks from the Devil, your great enemy. He prowls around like a roaring lion, looking for some victim to devour. Take a firm stand against him, and be strong in your faith. (NLT)

Prayer and Meditation

Psalm 5:3 - Morning by morning, O Lord, you hear my voice; morning by morning I lay my requests before you and wait in expectation.

Hebrews 4:16 - So let us come boldly to the throne of our gracious God. There we will receive his mercy, and we will find grace to help us when we need it. (NLT)

Philippians 4:8 - Fix your thoughts on what is true and honorable and right. Think about things that are pure and lovely and admirable. Think about things that are excellent and worthy of praise. (NLT)

James 5:16 - Therefore confess your sins to each other and pray for each other so that you may be healed. The prayer of a righteous man is powerful and effective.

Joshua 1:8 - Do not let this Book of the Law depart from your mouth; meditate on it day and night, so that you may be careful to do everything written in it. Then you will be prosperous and successful.

Psalm 1:1-2 - Blessed is the man who does not walk in the counsel of the wicked or stand in the way of sinners or sit in the seat of mockers. But his delight is in the law of the Lord, and on his law he meditates day and night.

Psalm 119:48 - I reach out my hands for your commandments, which I love, and I meditate on your decrees.

I Timothy 4:15 - Be diligent (meditate-*Greek*) in these matters; give yourself wholly to them, so that everyone may see your progress.

Seeking God

Psalm 42:1-2 - As the deer pants for streams of water, so my soul pants for you, O God. My soul thirsts for God, for the living God.

Isaiah 55:6 - Seek the Lord while he may be found; call on him while he is near.

Deuteronomy 4:29 - If you seek the Lord your God, you will find him—if you look for him with all your heart and with all your soul.

Matthew 7:8 - For everyone who asks receives; he who seeks finds; and to him who knocks, the door will be opened.

Psalm 119: 2, 10 – Blessed are they who keep his statutes and seek him with all their heart... I seek you with all my heart; do not let me stray from your commands.

II Chronicles 7:14 – If my people who are called by my name, will humble themselves and pray and seek my face and turn from their wicked ways, then will I hear from heaven and will forgive their sin and will heal their land.

Spiritual Battle

John 8:44 – You belong to your father, the devil, and you want to carry out your father's desire. He was a murderer from the beginning, not holding to the truth, for there is no truth in him. When he lies, he speaks his native language, for he is a liar and the father of lies.

John 10:10 – The thief comes only to steal and kill and destroy; I have come that they may have life, and have it to the full.

II Corinthians 11:14 – for Satan himself masquerades as an angel of light.

Ephesians 6:10-12 – Be strong with the Lord's mighty power. Put on all of God's armor, so that you will be able to stand firm against all strategies and tricks of the Devil. For we are not fighting against people made of flesh and blood, but against the evil rulers and authorities of the unseen world, against those mighty powers of darkness who rule this world, and against wicked spirits in the heavenly realms.

Ephesians 6:13-18 – Use every piece of God's armor to resist the enemy in the time of evil, so that after the battle you will still be standing firm. Stand your ground, putting on the sturdy belt of truth and the body armor of God's righteousness. For shoes, put on the peace that comes from the Good News, so that you will be fully prepared. In every battle you will need faith as your shield to stop the fiery arrows aimed at you by Satan. Put on salvation as your helmet, and take the sword of the Spirit, which is the word of God. Pray at all times and on every occasion in the power of the Holy Spirit. Stay alert and be persistent in your prayers for all Christians everywhere.

James 4:7-8 – Submit yourselves, then, to God. Resist the devil, and he will flee from you. Come near to God and he will come near to you.

Forgiveness

Matthew 6:14-15 – For when you forgive men when they sin against you, your heavenly Father will also forgive you. But if you do not forgive men their sins, your Father will not forgive your sins.

Matthew 18:21-22 – Then Peter came to Jesus and asked, "Lord, how many times shall I forgive my brother when he sins against me? Up to seven times?" Jesus answered, "I will tell you, not seven times, but seventy-seven times." *Read rest of chapter.*

Mark 11:25 – But when you are praying, first forgive anyone you are holding a grudge against, so that your Father in heaven will forgive your sins, too.

Ephesians 4:32 – Be kind and compassionate to one another, forgiving each other, just as in Christ God forgave you.

Hebrews 12:15 – See to it that no one misses the grace of God and that no bitter root grows up to cause trouble and defile many.

I John 1:9 – If we confess our sins, he is faithful and just and will forgive us our sins and purify us from all unrighteousness.

Renewal

Psalm 66:18 – If I had cherished sin in my heart, the Lord would not have listened.

Psalm 73:23-26 – Yet I am always with you; you hold me by my right hand. You guide me with your counsel, and afterward you will take me to glory. Whom have I in heaven but you? And being with you, I desire nothing on earth. My flesh and my heart may fail, but God is the strength of my heart and my portion forever.

Psalm 90:10, 12, 14, 17 - The length of our days is seventy years - or eighty, if we have the strength; yet the best of them is but trouble and sorrow, for they quickly pass, and we fly away... Teach us to number our days aright, that we may gain a heart of wisdom... Satisfy us in the morning with your unfailing love, that we may sing for joy and be glad all our days... May the favor of the Lord rest upon us; establish the work of our hands for us--yes, establish the work of our hands.

Psalm 119:11, 16, 18, 35-37 - I have hidden your word in my heart that I might not sin against you... I delight in your decrees; I will not neglect your word... Open my eyes that I may see wonderful things in your word... Direct me in the path of your commands, for there I find delight. Turn my heart toward your statutes and not toward selfish gain. Turn my eyes away from worthless things; renew my life according to your word.

Isaiah 40:30-31 - Even the youths grow tired and weary, and young men stumble and fall; but those who hope in the Lord will renew their strength. They will soar on wings like eagles; they will run and not grow weary, they will walk and not be faint.

Acts 3:19 - Repent, then, and turn to God, so that your sins may be wiped out, that times of refreshing may come from the Lord.

Psalm 37:7 - Be still before the Lord and wait patiently for him; do not fret when men succeed in their ways, when they carry out their wicked schemes.

II Corinthians 4:16-18 - That is why we never give up. Though our bodies are dying, our spirits are being renewed every day. For our present troubles are quite small and won't last very long. Yet they produce for us an immeasurably great glory that will last forever! So we don't look at the troubles we can see right now; rather, we look forward to what we have not yet seen. For the troubles we see will soon be over, but the joys to come will last forever. (NLT)

Ephesians 5:19-20 - Speak to one another with psalms, hymns and spiritual songs. Sing and make music in your heart to the Lord, always giving thanks to God the Father for everything.

Psalm 139:23-24 - Search me, O God, and know my heart; test me and know my anxious thoughts. See if there is any offensive way in me, and lead me in the way everlasting.

Promises

Psalm 34:19 - A righteous man may have many troubles, but the Lord delivers him from them all.

Ezekiel 36:26 - I will give you a new heart and put a new spirit in you; I will remove from you your heart of stone and give you a heart of flesh *(a new, obedient heart-NLT)*.

John 3:34 - God gives the Spirit without limit.

Galatians 3:28-29 - There is no longer Jew or Gentile, slave or free, male or female; for you are all Christians—you are one in Christ Jesus. And now that you belong to Christ, you are the true children of Abraham. You are his heirs, and now all the promises God gave to him belong to you. (NLT)

Ephesians 2:4-9 - God who is rich in mercy, made us alive in Christ even when we were dead in transgressions—it is by grace you have been saved, through faith...not of yourselves, it is a gift of God—not of works so that no one can boast.

Ephesians 3:20-21 - Now to him who is able to do immeasurably more than all we ask or imagine, according to his power that is at work within us, to him be the glory.

II Corinthians 12:9-10 - My grace is sufficient for you, for my power is made perfect in weakness... For when I am weak, then I am strong.

Godly Living

Psalm 143:8 – Let the morning bring me word of your unfailing love, for I have put my trust in you. Show me the way I should go, for to you I lift up my soul.

Psalm 141:3-4 – Set a guard over my mouth, O Lord, keep watch over the door of my lips. Let my heart not be drawn to what is evil.

Psalm 37:27 – Turn from evil and do good; then you will always live securely.

Philippians 1:27 – Whatever happens, conduct yourselves in a manner worthy of the gospel of Christ.

Isaiah 61:1-3 – The Spirit of the Sovereign Lord is on me, because the Lord has anointed me to preach the good news to the poor. He has sent me to bind up the broken hearted, proclaim freedom for the captives and release for the prisoners, and to proclaim the year of the Lord's favor, and to comfort all who mourn, and provide for those who grieve in Zion—to bestow on them a crown of beauty instead of ashes, the oil of gladness instead of mourning, a garment of praise instead of a spirit of despair.

Galatians 2:20 – I myself no longer live, but Christ lives in me. So I live my life in this earthly body by trusting in the Son of God, who loved me and gave himself for me. (NLT)

Galatians 5:13-14 – For you have been called to live in freedom—not freedom to satisfy your sinful nature, but freedom to serve one another in love. For the whole law can be summed up in this one command: "Love your neighbor as yourself." (NLT)

Galatians 5:16-18 – I advise you to live according to your new life in the Holy Spirit... And the Spirit gives us desires that are opposite from what the sinful nature desires. These two forces are constantly fighting each other, and your choices are never free from this conflict. But when you are directed by the Holy Spirit, you are no longer subject to the law. (NLT)

Galatians 5:22-23 - But when the Holy Spirit controls our lives, he will produce this kind of fruit in us: love, joy, peace, patience, kindness, goodness, faithfulness, gentleness, and self-control. (NLT)

Galatians 5:26 - Let us not become conceited, provoking and envying each other.

Galatians 6:2-3 - Share each other's troubles and problems, and in this way obey the law of Christ. If you think you are too important to help someone in need, you are only fooling yourself. You are really a nobody. (NLT)

Galatians 6:4-5 - Be sure to do what you should, for then you will enjoy the personal satisfaction of having done your work well, and you won't need to compare yourself to anyone else. For we are each responsible for our own conduct. (NLT)

Galatians 6:7-10 - Don't be misled. Remember that you can't ignore God and get away with it. You will always reap what you sow! ...Those who live to please the Spirit will harvest everlasting life from the Spirit. So don't get tired of doing what is good. Don't get discouraged and give up, for we will reap a harvest of blessing at the appropriate time. Whenever we have the opportunity, we should do good to everyone, especially to our Christian brothers and sisters. (NLT)

Ephesians 4:26-27 - In your anger do not sin: Do not let the sun go down while you are still angry, and do not give the devil a foothold.

Ephesians 4:2 - Be completely humble and gentle. Be patient with each other, making allowance for each other's faults because of your love. (NLT)

Ephesians 5:2 - Live a life of love.

Strength

Psalm 27:14 - Wait for the Lord; be strong and take heart and wait for the Lord.

Psalm 39:4-7 - Show me, O Lord, my life's end and the number of my days; let me know how fleeting is my life. You have made my days a mere handbreadth; the span of my years is as nothing before you... He bustles about, but only in vain; he heaps up wealth, not knowing who will get it. But now, Lord, what do I look for? My hope is in you.

Isaiah 12:2 - The Lord, the Lord, is my strength and my song; he has become my salvation.

Isaiah 41:10, 13 - For I am the Lord your God, who takes hold of your right hand and says to you, Do not fear; I will help you... So do not fear, for I am with you; do not be dismayed, for I am your God. I will strengthen you and help you; I will uphold you with my righteous right hand.

Ephesians 3:16-20 – I pray that out of his glorious riches he may strengthen you with power through his Spirit in your inner being, so that Christ may dwell in your hearts through faith. And I pray that you, being rooted and established in love, may have power, together with all the saints, to grasp how wide and long and high and deep is the love of Christ, and to know this love that surpasses knowledge—that you may be filled to the measure of all the fullness of God. Now to him who is able to do immeasurably more than all we ask or imagine, according to his power that is at work within us, to him be glory.

Nehemiah 8:10 - The joy of the Lord is your strength.

Comfort

Psalm 16:5-6 - Lord, you have assigned me my portion and my cup; you have made my lot secure. The boundary lines have fallen for me in pleasant places; surely I have a delightful inheritance.

Psalm 16:11 - You have made known to me the path of life; you will fill me with joy in your presence, with eternal pleasures at your right hand.

Psalm 63:7 - Because you are my help, I sing in the shadow of your wings.

Psalm 77:6 - I remember my songs in the night.

Psalm 91:1, 2, 14, 15 - He who dwells in the shelter of the Most High will rest in the shadow of the Almighty. I will say of the Lord, "He is my refuge and my fortress, my God, in whom I trust." "Because he loves me," says the Lord, "I will rescue him; I will protect him, for he acknowledges my name. He will call upon me, and I will answer him; I will be with him in trouble, I will deliver him and honor him."

Psalm 138:8 - The Lord will fulfill his purpose for me; your love, O Lord, endures forever—do not abandon the works of your hands.

Isaiah 14:24, 27 - Surely, as I have planned, so will it be, and as I have purposed, so it will stand... For the Lord Almighty has purposed, and who can thwart him? His hand is stretched out and who can turn it back?

Isaiah 49:15-16 - Can a mother forget the baby at her breast, and have no compassion on the child she has born? Though she may forget, I will never forget you! See, I have engraved you on the palms of my hands.

Isaiah 64:4 - For since the world began, no ear has heard, and no eye has seen a God like you, who works for those who wait for him! (NLT)

Philippians 1:6 - Being confident of this, that he who began a good work in you will carry it on to completion until the day of Christ Jesus.

Philippians 4:19 - And my God will meet all your needs according to his glorious riches in Christ Jesus.

Encouragement

Psalm 138:3 - When I pray, you answer me; you encourage me by giving me the strength I need. (NLT)

Psalm 139:3-5, 13-14, 16 - You are familiar with all my ways. Before a word is on my tongue you know it completely, O Lord. You hem me in—behind and before; you have laid your hand upon me... For you created my inmost being; you knit me together in my mother's womb. I praise you because I am fearfully and wonderfully made... All the days ordained for me were written in your book before one of them came to be.

Psalm 102:19-20 - The Lord looked down from his sanctuary on high, from heaven he viewed the earth, to hear the groans of the prisoners and release those condemned to death.

Isaiah 43:18-19 - Forget the former things; do not dwell on the past. See, I am doing a new thing! Now it springs up; do you not perceive it?

Galations 1:15 - It pleased God in his kindness to choose me and call me, even before I was born! What undeserved mercy! *(Paul then obeyed God's call)* (NLT)

Ephesians 1:17-19 - I keep asking that the God of our Lord Jesus Christ, the glorious Father, may give you the Spirit of wisdom and revelation, so that you may know him better. I pray also that the eyes of your heart may be enlightened in order that you may know the hope to which he has called you, the riches of his glorious inheritance in you, and his incomparably great power for us who believe. That power is like the working of his mighty strength, which he exerted in Christ when he raised him from the dead and seated him at his right hand.

Lamentations 3:22-26 - Because of the Lord's great love we are not consumed, for his compassions never fail. They are new every morning; great is your faithfulness. I say to myself, "The Lord is my portion; therefore I will wait for him." The Lord is good to those whose hope is in him, to the one who seeks him; it is good to wait quietly for the salvation of the Lord.

Lamentations 3:32-33 - Though he brings grief, he will show compassion, so great is his unfailing love. For he does not willingly bring affliction or grief to the children of men.

Galatians 3:14 - Through the work of Christ Jesus, God has blessed the Gentiles with the same blessing he promised to Abraham, and we Christians receive the promised Holy Spirit through faith.

Galatians 4:3-7 - Before Christ came, we were slaves to the spiritual powers of this world. But when the right time came, God sent his Son, born of a woman, subject to the law. God sent him to buy freedom for us who were slaves to the law, so that he could adopt us as his very own children. And because you Gentiles have become his children, God has sent the Spirit of his Son into your hearts, and now you can call God your dear Father. Now you are no longer a slave but God's own child. And since you are his child, everything he has belongs to you.

Ephesians 1:3 - We have been blessed in the heavenly realms with every spiritual blessing in Christ.

Ephesians 1:4, 5, 7, 8, 13, 14 - Long ago, even before he made the world, God loved us and chose us in Christ to be holy and without fault in his eyes. His unchanging plan has always been to adopt us into his own family by bringing us to himself through Jesus Christ. And this gave him great pleasure... He is so rich in kindness that he purchased our freedom through the blood of his Son, and our sins are forgiven. He has showered his kindness on us, along with all wisdom and understanding... And now you also have heard the truth, the Good News that God saves you. And when you believed in Christ, he identified you as his own by giving you the Holy Spirit, whom he promised long ago. The Spirit is God's guarantee that he will give us everything he promised and that he has purchased us to be his own people. This is just one more reason for us to praise our glorious God. (NLT)

Ephesians 2:10 - For we are God's masterpiece. He has created us anew in Christ Jesus, so that we can do the good things he planned for us long ago. (NLT)

Hope

Ephesians 1:18-19 - I pray also that the eyes of your heart may be enlightened in order that you may know the hope to which God has called you, the riches of his glorious inheritance in the saints, and his incomparably great power for us who believe.

Psalm 62:5 - Find rest, O my soul, in God alone; my hope comes from him.

Proverbs 23:18 - There is surely a future hope for you, and your hope will not be cut off.

Hebrews 4:16 - Let us then approach the throne of grace with confidence, so that we may receive mercy and find grace to help us in our time of need.

Psalm 9:10 - Those who know your name will trust in you, for you, Lord, have never forsaken those who seek you.

Romans 15:13 - May the God of hope fill you with all joy and peace as you trust in him, so that you may overflow with hope by the power of the Holy Spirit.

Romans 5:5 - Hope does not disappoint us because God has poured out his love into our hearts by the Holy Spirit, whom he has given us.

Micah 7:7 - I watch in hope for the Lord, I wait for God my Savior; my God will hear me.

Proverbs 23:18 - There is surely a future hope for you, and your hope will not be cut off.

Trust

Psalm 62:8 - Trust in him at all times; pour out your hearts to him, for God is our refuge.

Psalm 56:3 - But when I am afraid, I put my trust in you. (NLT)

Psalm 28:7 - The Lord is my strength, my shield from every danger. I trust in him with all my heart. He helps me, and my heart is filled with joy. I burst out in songs of thanksgiving. (NLT)

Psalm 13:5-6 – I trust in your unfailing love. I will rejoice because you have rescued me. I will sing to the Lord because he has been so good to me. (NLT)

Psalm 9:10 – Those who know your name trust in you, for you, O Lord, have never abandoned anyone who searches for you. (NLT)

Psalm 32:10 – Many sorrows come to the wicked, but unfailing love surrounds those who trust the Lord. (NLT)

Psalm 146:3 – Don't put your confidence in powerful people; there is no help for you there. (NLT)

Jeremiah 17:7-8 – Blessed are those who trust in the Lord and have made the Lord their hope and confidence. They are like trees planted along a riverbank, with roots that reach deep into the water. Such trees are not bothered by the heat or worried by long months of drought. Their leaves stay green, and they go right on producing delicious fruit. (NLT)

Psalm 37:5 – Commit everything you do to the Lord. Trust him, and he will help you. (NLT)

Breaking Strongholds through Prayer

Predispositions	God's Opposites	Scriptures to Write Out, Pray and Meditate On
Unworthy	Valued	Romans 8:1-2, Isaiah 49:16, Jeremiah 31:3
Anger	Forgiveness	Matthew 6:12-15, 18:21-22; Mark 11:25
	Love	Proverbs 10:12; Matthew 5:43-44, 46; John 13:34-35; I John 4:18
Fear, Anxiety	Trust God	Philippians 4:6-7; I Peter 5:7-9
	Peace	John 14:27; Isaiah 26:3

The above are examples. List your personal Predispositions and find the Scriptures for God's opposites on which to meditate and pray.

Freedom from Sexual Partners

In the name of Jesus Christ by the power of his cross and blood, we take the sword of the Spirit and cut _____ free from all previous sexual partners. We especially cut _____ free from _____, _____, _____, _____, _____, _____. (First names or initials)

We cut him/her free from these people physically, spiritually, emotionally and mentally. We not only cut him/her free from these people, Lord, but we cut him/her free from anyone and everyone he/she has ever had sex with also.

We place the cross and blood of Jesus between _____ and each of these people. We pray for a cleansing and purification of _____'s mind, body and spirit; that he/she may walk in wholeness, purification and redemption.

Fill _____ with the power of your Holy Spirit that he/she may walk in your abundant grace and mercy.

Fill him/her Lord with your love, that it may permeate all dark and lonely places. Most of all Lord, help _____ to know how much you love him/her and how special he/she is to you.

Prayer of Repentance

Lord Jesus, I know I have sinned against you by choosing a lifestyle that is not pleasing to you. I have rebelled against you in many ways. Because of my rebellion, I have brought destruction into my life and the lives of others. I repent of this. As an act of my will, I turn from my evil ways and thoughts and turn to you for your help since I am unable to help myself. I renounce my lifestyle of sinful thoughts and behaviors. In all your compassion, have mercy on me. Through the power of the Holy Spirit, enable me to become all that you created me to be.

I have defiled my flesh and spirit in such a way that it is an abomination to you. I have led such an ungodly life by following the ways of this world and worshipping the Satanic spirits of lust, self-indulgence, greed and all darkness that satisfied my depraved nature. I repent of: _____

_____

_____

I desire to be united with you my creator and redeemer. I no longer desire to lead a double life—pretending to be someone that I am not. I desire to have a singleness of spirit that is united with your Spirit. I desire to have the "mind of Christ."

Lord I truly repent of all these sins in my life: _____

_____

_____

Wash me clean with the blood of Jesus. Begin your work of healing in the very depths of my heart. Make known to me who you created me to be. "Create in me a clean heart and renew a right spirit within me," a spirit that will worship you, glorify you and serve you for the rest of my life.

In the name of Jesus Christ, I pray this prayer and make this whole-hearted commitment to you, Holy Father. I also ask that you anoint me with your Holy Spirit and send your ministering angels to surround me and minister to my needs in order that these desires of my heart may come to fruition in my life. My deepest desire is to "live to the praise of your glory." I praise you, Father, Son and Holy Spirit for what you are doing and will do in my life to bring me to wholeness in you. Amen

Prayer to Break Any Curse on Your Life

(especially if the curse has been a result of occult involvement)

Lord Jesus Christ, I believe that you are the Son of God and the only way to God, and that you died on the cross for my sins and rose again from the dead.

I give up all my rebellion and all my sin, and I submit myself to you as my Lord. I confess all my sins before you and ask for your forgiveness—especially for any sins that exposed me to a curse. Release me also from the consequences of my ancestors' sins.

By a decision of my will, I forgive all who have harmed me or wronged me—just as I want God to forgive me. In particular, I forgive [name individuals].

I renounce all contact with anything occult or satanic—if I have any "contact objects," I commit myself to destroy them. I cancel all Satan's claims against me.

Lord Jesus, I believe that on the cross you took on yourself every curse that could ever come upon me. So I ask you now to release me from every curse over my life—in your name, Lord Jesus Christ! By faith, I now receive my release and thank you for it (From *Blessing or Curse—You Can Choose* by Derek Prince).

This prayer, with slight adaption, could also be prayed by all those wanting to turn their lives over to Jesus Christ, realizing that without salvation, we are all under a curse for our sins. John 3:16 tells us, *"For God so loved the world that He gave His one and only Son, that whoever believes in Him shall not perish but have eternal life."*

Prayer for Protection

(to be said prior to ministry)

In the name of Jesus Christ and by the power of his cross and his blood, we bind up the power of any evil spirits and command them not to block our prayers. We bind up the powers of earth, air, water, fire, the netherworld, and the satanic forces of nature.

We break any curses, hexes, or spells sent against us and declare them null and void. We break the assignments of any spirits sent against us and send them to Jesus to deal with as he will. Lord, we ask you to bless our enemies by sending your Holy Spirit to lead them to repentance and conversion.

Furthermore, we bind all interaction and communication in the world of evil spirits as it affects us and our ministry.

We ask for the protection of the shed blood of Jesus Christ over _____.

Thank you, Lord, for your protection and send your angels to help us in the battle. We ask you to guide us in our prayers; share with us your Spirit's power and compassion. Amen.

Note: "Earth, air, fire and water" are unfamiliar categories to most of us, but they are used by Satanists in casting curses. We are simply breaking curses by reversing them in the same terms that Satanists use.

Appendix C

A RANDOMIZED TRIAL OF THE EFFECT OF PRAYER ON DEPRESSION AND ANXIETY*

PETER A. BOELENS, MD, MPH
University of Mississippi and Shalom Prayer Ministry

ROY R. REEVES, DO, PH.D.
Jackson VA Medical Center and University of Mississippi

WILLIAM H. REPLOGLE, PH.D.
University of Mississippi Medical Center

HAROLD G. KOENIG, MD
*Duke University Medical Center and
VA Medical Center, Durham, North Carolina*

ABSTRACT

Objective: To investigate the effect of direct contact person-to-person prayer on depression, anxiety, positive emotions, and salivary cortisol levels. *Design, Setting, and Participants:* Cross-over clinical trial with depression or anxiety conducted in an office setting. Following randomization to the prayer intervention or control groups, subjects (95% women) completed Hamilton Rating Scales for Depression and Anxiety, Life Orientation Test, Daily Spiritual Experiences Scale, and underwent measurement of cortisol levels. Individuals in the direct person-to-person prayer contact intervention group received six weekly 1-hour prayer sessions while those in the control group received none. Rating scales and cortisol levels were repeated for both groups after completion of the prayer sessions, and a month later. ANOVAs

*The cortisol analysis was funded by The Luke Society, Inc., 3409 Gateway Blvd., Sioux Falls, SD, a worldwide charitable medical organization.

were used to compare pre- and post-prayer measures for each group. *Results:* At the completion of the trial, participants receiving the prayer intervention showed significant improvement of depression and anxiety, as well as increases of daily spiritual experiences and optimism compared to controls ($p < 0.01$ in all cases). Subjects in the prayer group maintained these significant improvements ($p < 0.01$ in all cases) for a duration of at least 1 month after the final prayer session. Participants in the control group did not show significant changes during the study. Cortisol levels did not differ significantly between intervention and control groups, or between pre- and post-prayer conditions. *Conclusions:* Direct contact person-to-person prayer may be useful as an adjunct to standard medical care for patients with depression and anxiety. Further research in this area is indicated.

(*Int'l. J. Psychiatry in Medicine* 2009;39:377-392)

Key Words: depression, anxiety, direct person-to-person prayer, emotions, neuroplasticity

Depression and anxiety are closely linked disorders of emotion. At any given time, 10% of the United States population has been affected by depression and 18% by an anxiety disorder in the previous year [1, 2]. This translates into primary care physicians seeing at least one person with significant depression or anxiety every day that they practice. When disability is measured as "time in bed" depression ranks higher than lung disease, diabetes, or arthritis and is surpassed only by heart disease [3]. Depression is a common cause of extended work absence among employees [4] and as a disorder of emotion, it often complicates other acute and chronic diseases, adversely affecting both patient recovery and longevity [5]. According to a World Health Organization, depression will place the second largest burden of ill health worldwide by the year 2020 [6, 7].

All participants in this trial had depression while most others had anxiety or symptoms of anxiety. They represented the demographics of the area with a mix of Protestant, Pentecostal, Catholic, and non-denominational with the group consisting of women with only three males. All participants exhibited spirituality in that they spoke of daily prayers asking God for healing which did not necessarily correlate with religious practices such as church involvement.

There have been numerous studies demonstrating the effect of religious practices serving as a coping behavior in mental diseases such as depression and anxiety. In the majority of these cases the effect has been positive [8]. In our search of the literature, however, we were unable to document any clinical trials of person-to-person prayer in the field of mental illness published in a peer-reviewed journal. Most previous studies of prayer have examined the effect of prayer over *distance* on various physical health outcomes (i.e., remote intercessory prayer) [9-11]. A systematic review of 23 trials involving 2774 participants evaluating the efficacy of any form of "distant healing" as treatment for any medical condition showed that 13 trials (57%) yielded statistically significant treatment effects, 9 trials showed no effect over control interventions, and 1 showed a negative effect [12]. However, a meta-analysis of 14 studies of distant prayer for healing suggested no discernable effect [13] and a review of 10 studies (7646 subjects) of intercessory prayer for a variety of health conditions concluded that the results could not be interpreted with any degree of confidence [14]. Direct contact prayer on a person-to-person basis with the "laying on of hands," however, has been associated with enhanced participant well being [15] and clinical improvement of individuals with chronic rheumatoid arthritis [16]. The prayers in this study were person-to-person prayers without physical contact. They differ from intercessory prayers in that there is no intercession to God for the healing of depression and/or anxiety but rather they were prayers going back in time asking for God's healing of life stressors combined with prayers of forgiveness. Both of these prayers result in a separation of traumatic memories from their corresponding negative emotions. In addition, various form prayers were utilized where appropriate. Furthermore, with these prayers there exists a mechanism within the scientific framework to explain how such effects might come about.

Realizing that depression is a chronic illness for which antidepressant drugs do not provide a long-term cure, that it is the most prevalent mental disorder for which individuals are least likely to seek treatment, and that 35% of Americans use prayer to address health-related issues [17] such as these, we investigated the effect of prayers over time conducted on a *person-to-person* basis by a Christian lay prayer minister. These prayers address the underlying causes of depression and anxiety which in many instances are life traumas and stressors that have occurred in the distant past as well as the present. We hypothesize that these prayers will lessen depression and anxiety, enhance positive emotions such as hope and spirituality, and lower salivary cortisol.

METHODS

This randomized cross-over trial was conducted between September 2005 and May 2008 in an outpatient setting in Vicksburg, Mississippi. Institutional Review Board approval was obtained through Copernicus Group IRB, Research Triangle Park, North Carolina.

Measurements

All participants in the study met DSM-IV-TR criteria for depressive disorder [18]. Most also had symptoms of anxiety. The severity of symptoms was measured utilizing the Hamilton Depression Rating Scale (HDRS) [19] with a score of 10 or more and the Hamilton Anxiety Rating Scales (HARS) [20] with a score of 17 or more. The Life Orientation Test (LOT) [21] measured the effects of dispositional optimism on self-regulation in a variety of circumstances. There are eight questions, with the highest score (most optimism) being 32. It has shown construct validity with other studies demonstrating the effect of optimism in health promotion in a variety of circumstances [21]. The Daily Spiritual Experiences Scale (DSES) [22] used 16 questions to measure spiritual experience such as awe, joy, and a sense of inner peace, with the highest score (least spiritual) being 94 and the lowest score (most spiritual) being 16. The DSES evidences good reliability across several scales.

Participants

Participants were individuals aged 18 or older who exhibited depression and/or anxiety. Individuals were excluded if they had any chronic disease or evidence of cognitive impairment, if they had received steroidal medication within the preceding 2 months, or if they had been treated with psychotherapy during the preceding year. If subjects were taking antidepressants or antianxiety medications, the dosages of these medications remained unchanged throughout the duration of the study.

Participants were recruited from medical physician offices through posters placed in the waiting area and examination rooms. Respondents included 60 females and 3 males. It is unclear why the majority of respondents were female. Referral was made by either the clinic physician or nurse. There was no direct advertisement of the study in the community. However, as the study became visible in the community, some individuals presented requesting enrollment. The demographics of study participants are displayed in Table 1.

Table 1. Demographics[a]

	Control participants (n = 36)	Prayer participants (n = 27)
Sex		
Male n (%)	2 (5.6)	1 (3.7)
Female n (%)	34 (94.4)	26 (96.3)
Race		
African-American n (%)	23 (63.9)	13 (48.1)
Caucasian n (%)	13 (36.1)	14 (51.9)
Age – mean years (sd)	43.3 (14.0)	44.4 (12.5)
Hamilton D > 9 n (%)	36 (100)	27 (100)
Hamilton A > 16 n (%)	22 (61.1)	19 (70.4)

[a]All between group comparisons, $p > 0.05$.

Study Design

After providing informed consent, participants were administered the HDRS, HARS, LOT, and DSES. They were given sample tubes for collection of salivary specimens for cortisol measurements at 8 A.M., Noon, 5 P.M., and 9 P.M. Subjects were randomized into a prayer intervention group or a control group (Figure 1). (There was a higher dropout rate among controls than among the intervention group. To compensate for this, the randomization program was weighted toward more controls.) A series of six weekly prayer intervention sessions were begun for the prayer intervention group. When the prayer sessions were completed, the scales were again administered and the salivary samples collected for cortisol analysis.

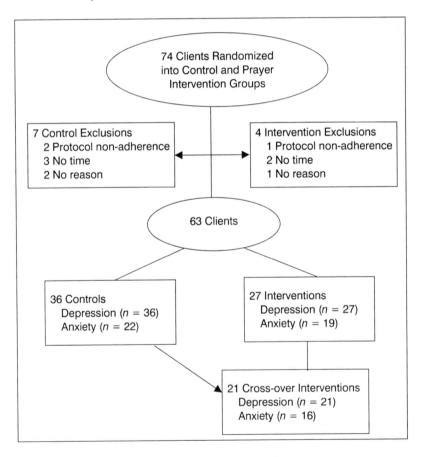

Figure 1. Prayer study profile.

The control group received no prayer or any other intervention during the 6 weeks when the prayer group was receiving prayers. Scales were administered and salivary cortisols were collected before and after the 6 weeks. After serving as controls for the prayer intervention group, they were eligible to cross over to participate in prayer intervention and receive prayers following the same protocol as the prayer intervention group. Because of scheduling difficulties, the last five control cross-over subjects entering the study received only five of the six prayer intervention sessions.

After the six prayer sessions for both the intervention and crossed-over control group, there was no prayer intervention during the following month or any other counseling, psychotherapy, or medication changes. At the end of that month clients were again administered the rating scales and salivary samples were collected as before. All scoring and cortisol collection was done by a single clinician unblinded as to group assignment.

Prayer Intervention

All prayer interventions were conducted by a single lay prayer minister who was a non-denominational Caucasian college graduate in her late sixties with prayer training by Christian Healing Ministries (Jacksonville, FL). A distance was maintained from the client so as to avoid touching through a hand shake or any other physical contact. A history was taken in order to delineate particular areas for prayer. There was no psychotherapy, however, causing participants to gain insights into their problems. Direct person-to-person prayer was the only intervention. The prayers utilized were determined by the lay prayer minister and based on the history of the participant. During the prayer sessions, the prayer minister prayed and was often joined by the participant in praying various form prayers, prayers releasing hurts, and prayers of blessings on those who had offended them.

The first prayer session was 90 minutes in duration and involved determination of the subject's issues to be addressed by prayer. The remaining sessions were 60 minutes each and were tailored to the individual participant's needs. Sessions included prayer about specific stressors and, when needed, for childhood traumas and for repentance of behavior. In cases of emotional difficulty related to traumatic memories, prayers asking that God come into the memories and heal were provided.

Statistical Analysis

Demographic characteristics of the control and prayer groups were compared using a chi-square test for nominal variables and an independent *t*-test for interval variables.

For each dependent variable, we tested for differences in the baseline assessment between the prayer intervention group and the control group. We then performed for each dependent variable an analysis of covariance (ANCOVA) with the 6-week post-intervention assessment as the dependent variable, group membership (prayer versus control) as the independent variable, and the respective baseline measurement as the covariate. We then performed separately for the prayer intervention group, the crossover prayer intervention group, and the combined prayer and crossover prayer group a one-way repeated measures ANOVA with the baseline, post-prayer intervention, and 1-month follow-up measures as the three dependent variables. Significant ANOVAs were followed by Bonferroni adjusted pair-wise comparisons of the three assessments. An alpha level of 0.05 was used to determine statistical significance.

RESULTS

There was no statistical difference between the control and intervention groups in terms of sex, race, age in years, or prevalence of depression or anxiety (Table 1). Baseline, 6-week post-intervention, and 1-month post-intervention follow-up measurements are shown in Table 2. For each dependent measure, we failed to find a significant difference between the control and prayer intervention baseline measures. The ANCOVAs using the HDRS, HARS, Life Orientation Test, and Daily Spiritual Experiences Scale as dependent variables indicated significant differences between the prayer intervention and the control groups. The prayer intervention group had significantly lower mean post-intervention HDRS (Figure 2), HARS (Figure 3), and Daily Spiritual Experiences Scale scores (Figure 4) and a significantly higher mean Life Orientation Test score (Figure 5). The ANCOVA for salivary cortisol was non-significant.

For the prayer intervention group, the control crossover intervention group, and the combined prayer and crossover prayer group, separately, the repeated measures ANOVAs using the HDRS, HARS, Life Orientation Test, and Daily Spiritual Experiences Scale as dependent variables resulted in significant within-group differences. Bonferroni adjusted pairwise comparisons indicated that there were significant decreases in mean HDRS, HARS, and Daily Spiritual Experiences Scale scores from baseline to post-intervention and from baseline to 1-month post-intervention follow-up. There were significant increases in mean in the Life Orientation Test scores from baseline to post-intervention and from baseline to 1-month post-intervention follow-up. The data with males in or out of the study was analyzed without statistically significant differences in outcomes. The repeated measures ANOVAs using salivary cortisol as the dependent measure were non-significant.

Table 2. Mean Responses of Control and Prayer Groups
Mean (Standard deviation)

	Baseline	Post intervention	1-Month follow-up
Hamilton Depression Scale			
Control (n = 36)	22.72 (5.1)	22.56 (5.6)	
Prayer (n = 48)	23.29 (5.6)	6.46 (4.6)*†	5.83 (4.3)†
Prayer Intervention (n = 27)	22.63 (5.9)	6.22 (4.8)*†	5.63 (3.8)†
Crossover Intervention (n = 21)	24.14 (5.2)	6.76 (4.5)*†	6.10 (4.9)†
Hamilton Anxiety Scale			
Control (n = 22)	23.50 (6.0)	23.77 (8.1)	
Prayer (n = 35)	25.06 (7.0)	4.80 (4.9)*†	4.49 (5.9)†
Prayer Intervention (n = 27)	25.37 (5.4)	4.26 (4.8)*†	3.42 (4.6)†
Crossover Intervention (n = 21)	24.69 (8.8)	5.44 (5.0)*†	5.75 (7.1)†
Life Orientation Test			
Control (n = 36)	16.19 (6.2)	16.19 (5.8)	
Prayer (n = 48)	16.73 (6.0)	24.00 (5.2)*†	24.83 (5.4)†
Prayer Intervention (n = 27)	17.04 (6.8)	24.11 (5.0)*†	25.33 (4.7)†
Crossover Intervention (n = 21)	16.33 (n = 4.9)	23.86 (5.6)*†	24.19 (6.4)†

Daily Spiritual Experiences Scale			
Control (n = 36)	47.39 (15.2)	44.56 (16.1)	28.67 (10.8)†
Prayer (n = 48)	43.46 (14.8)	28.46 (9.5)*†	27.07 (9.4)†
Prayer Intervention (n = 27)	40.74 (14.5)	26.52 (7.8)*†	30.71 (12.3)†
Crossover Intervention (n = 21)	46.95 (14.7)	30.95 (11.0)*†	
Salivary Cortisol Concentration			
Control (n = 31)	5.17 (14.4)	2.91 (1.7)	3.06 (1.2)
Prayer (n = 48)	2.80 (1.0)	3.73 (6.1)	3.24 (1.2)
Prayer Intervention (n = 27)	3.11 (1.1)	4.59 (8.0)	2.82 (1.2)
Crossover Intervention (n = 21)	2.42 (0.8)	2.61 (0.9)	

*$p < 0.05$ versus Control Group ANCOVA.
†For one-way within subjects ANOVA, $p < 0.01$. Bonferroni adjusted pairwise comparisons indicate Baseline is significantly different from Post-intervention and 1-Month follow-up, $p < 0.01$.

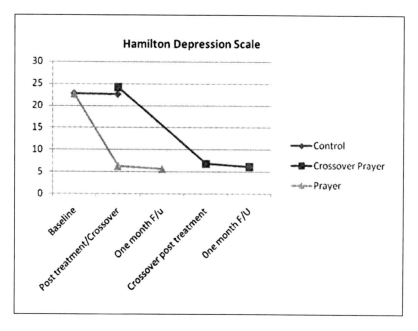

Figure 2. Hamilton Depression Scale values.
< 10–13 Mild; 14–17 Mild to moderate; > 17 Moderate to severe.

DISCUSSION

These findings supported our hypothesis that these prayers significantly lower the level of depression and anxiety while they concomitantly elevate the level of optimism and spirituality. We were surprised, however, that these changes were not reflected in the cortisol AUC concentrations. The AUC cortisol measurement is considered the most significant measure linking cortisol levels and psychological functioning [23]. One would have expected the AUC cortisol levels to decrease after prayer intervention. We have no cogent reason as to why these prayers had no effect on cortisol levels and yet exerted a significant effect on the level of depression and anxiety. Perhaps this occurred because of either daily variability in cortisol levels brought on by common stressors in life [24] or that healing might be related to the participants' perceptions.

Attempting to understand why there was such a dramatic improvement of depression and anxiety with a concomitant rise in optimism and spirituality among participants in this study, we reviewed the Hamilton D item #2 where 47% of participants with depression and 44% of participants with anxiety related feelings of self-reproach and guilt and ruminated over past errors. This was postulated to create a milieu of self-devaluative negativity and hopelessness which

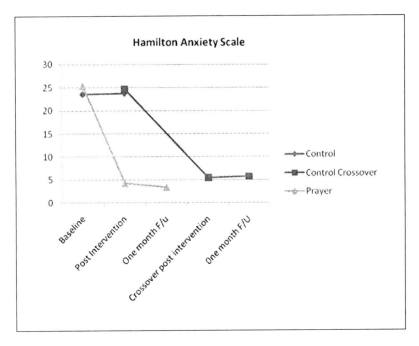

Figure 3. Hamilton Anxiety Scale values.
< 17 Mild or None; 18–24 Mild to Moderate; 25–30 Moderate to Severe.

in turn promulgates thought patterns that had the potential to both cause and perpetuate depression and anxiety [25]. We postulate that prayer intervention can help alleviate this vicious cycle.

Research has demonstrated that in successful psychotherapy for depression there is not only a change in thought content but also its relationship to negativity. This distancing from negative thoughts or "decentering" is accomplished through "mindfulness therapy" [25] which find its roots in Buddhist meditation. In this study, prayers removed the negative emotions and facilitated a "decentering" in an effective and speedy way. As the participants focused on Scriptures, they were able to build positive emotions with concomitant thought patterns.

Forgiveness prayers and prayers asking God to come into traumatic memories served to separate the traumatic memories from their associated negative emotions. The memory exists but as an isolated incident without emotional connections. Participants have described the occurrence as if someone had "removed the trigger from the gun"—the gun being the memory, and the trigger the emotions. When asked to reconnect to the memory and their emotions, they

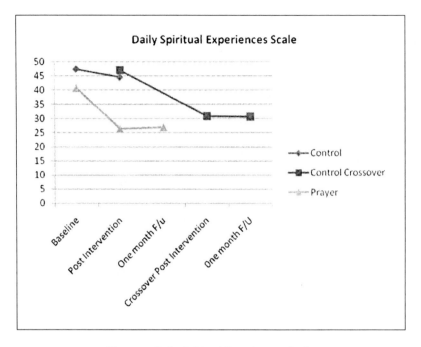

Figure 4. Daily Spiritual Experiences Scale.
An increased numerical score correlates with a decrease in spirituality
and closeness to God. The highest score (least spiritual) is 94 and
the lowest score (most spiritual) is 16.

reconnect with ease to the memory but were unable to connect with any associated emotions. The memory stands as a fact of life without emotional significance.

This is important from a psychotherapeutic perspective. Conscious cognitive thoughts give us a choice of actions to be taken, but the unconscious emotional appraisal system limits these choices to those that are appropriate to the given situation [26]. Our rational decision making is processed by our emotions. When negative emotions are unlinked from hurtful memories, it is postulated that participants are freed from their compromised emotional appraisal system and are no longer bothered by triggering events unleashing a cascade of hormones and old thought patterns that are so frequently experienced by some patients. It is postulated that without triggering events or the limitation of a compromised emotional appraisal system, unhealthy thought patterns can be changed with much less effort and greater success.

Studies utilizing neuroimaging have shown how the pathologic thought patterns and associated behavior can be changed through directed and attentive

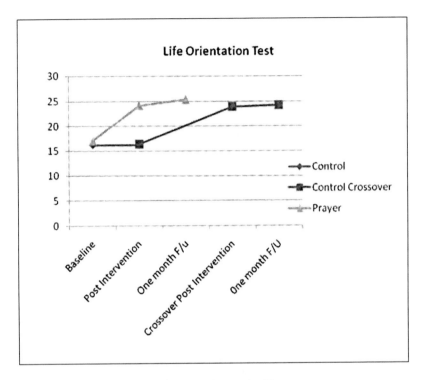

Figure 5. Life Orientation Test.
An increase in the numerical score correlates with an increase in optimism.
The highest score (most optimism) is 32 and the lowest is 0.

mental effort [27]. This has become known as "self-directed" neuroplasticity. Subjects engaged in this directed and attentive mental effort throughout the day in the form of prayers, in most instances begin experiencing changes in thought patterns and emotions in a matter of weeks. It is our hypothesis that clients continuing this practice would remain depression and anxiety free.

There is a system in the brain of mice that utilizes positive emotions [28]. This is a system connecting the amygdala, striatum, and prefrontal cortex. This system not only enhances feelings of contentment and safety (positive emotions) but also reduces fear (negative emotions). This has led Kandel to make the observation, "Therapies that enhance the neural circuitry for safety and well-being might well provide a more effective approach to treating anxiety disorders" [29], and to this we add depression. Participants in this study experienced a touch of the transcendent for which science has no tools to measure, but its reflection was seen in a marked increase in optimism and spirituality. It is postulated that their neural circuitry for well-being was greatly enhanced through these prayers. Today, with neuroimaging we have the capability of exploring how this system works in the human brain.

LIMITATIONS

This study is limited by the fact that it was not blinded and a sham control group was not utilized. There was selection bias in the study in that individuals desiring prayer were self-referred through posters in physicians' offices and by word of mouth. This selection process resulted in 95% women. As a result, the findings cannot be generalized to men who remained in the study because their data did not alter the outcome measurements. The study was conducted in the "Bible-belt" of the United States and represented the demographics of the area (a denominational mix of Christians) which make the results of this study non-transferable to other beliefs. The numbers were insufficient for subgroup analysis, and data on income and educational level was not collected.

CONCLUSION

Despite the study's limitations, it opens the door to further investigations utilizing PET and fMRI to delineate what is occurring in the brain as hurtful emotions are separated from traumatic memories, positive emotions are released, and clients intentionally activate a form of prayerful self-directed neuroplasticity. There are now studies delineating brain functioning that document the effects of drug and psychotherapy in depression utilizing PET and fMRI [30]. These same imaging tools can be utilized to evaluate the effect of prayer. If the effects of these prayers are maintained over time, it is reasonable to conclude that there will be structural changes in the brain. The knowledge gained through this study needs replication and expansion through future studies.

REFERENCES

1. Kessler RC, McGonagle KA, Zhao S, et al. Lifetime and twelve-month prevalence of DSM-III-R psychiatric disorders in the United States: Results from the National Comorbidity Study. *Archives of General Psychiatry* 1994;51:8-19.
2. Kessler RC, Chiu WT, Demler O, et al. Prevalence, severity, and comorbidity of twelve-month DSM-IV disorders in the National Comorbidity Survey Replication (NCS-R). *Archives of General Psychiatry* 2005;62:617-627.
3. Wells KB, Sturm R, Sherbourne CD, et al. *Caring for depression.* Boston: Harvard University Press, 1998.
4. Broadhead WE, Blazer DG, et al. Depression, disability days, and days lost from work in a prospective epidemiologic survey. *The Journal of the American Medical Association* 1990;264(19):2524-2528.

5. Connerney I, Shapiro PA, McLaughlin JS, et al. Relation between depression after coronary artery bypass surgery and 12 month outcome: A prospective study. *Lancet* 2001;358:1766-1771.

6. Murray CL, Lopez AD. *The global burden of disease: A comprehensive assessment of mortality and disability from disease, risk factors in 1990 and projected to 2020.* Boston: Harvard University Press; 1998.

7. WHO/The global burden of disease: 2004; Part 3, Disease incidence, prevalence and disability: 36.

8. Koenig HG. Research on religion, spirituality, and mental health: A review. *The Canadian Journal of Psychiatry* 2009;54(5):283-291.

9. Byrd RC. Positive therapeutic effects of intercessory prayer in a coronary care unit population. *Southern Medical Journal* 1988;81:826-829.

10. Harris WS, Gowda M, Kolb JW, et al. A randomized, controlled trial of the effects of remote, intercessory prayer on outcomes in patients admitted to the coronary care unit. *Archives of Internal Medicine* 1999;159:2273-2278.

11. Benson H, Dusek JA, Sherwood JB, et al. Study of the therapeutic effects of intercessory prayer in cardiac bypass patients: A multicenter randomized trial of uncertainty and certainty of receiving intercessory prayer. *American Heart Journal* 2006;151(4):934-936.

12. Astin JA, Harkness E, Ernst E. The efficacy of "distant healing: A systematic review of randomized trials. *Annals of Internal Medicine* 2000;132:903-910.

13. Masters KS, Spielmans GI, Goodson JT. Are there demonstrable effects of distant intercessory prayer? A meta-analytic review. *Annals of Behavioral Medicine* 2006; 32:21-26.

14. *Cochrane Database of Systematic Reviews* 2007, Issue 1. Art No.: CD000368. DOI: 10.1002/14651858.CD000368.pub2.

15. Beutler JJ, Attevelt JTM, Schouten S, et al. Paranormal healing and hypertension. *British Medical Journal* 1988;296:1491-1492.

16. Matthews DA, Marlowe SM, MacNutt FS. Effects of intercessory prayer on patients with rheumatoid arthritis. *Southern Medical Journal* 2000;93(12):1117-1186.

17. Eisenberg DM, Davis RB, Ettner SL, et al. Trends in alternative medicine used in the United States, 1990-1997: results of a follow-up national survey. *The Journal of the American Medical Association* 1998;280:1569-1575.

18. American Psychiatric Association. Diagnostic and Statistical Manual of Mental Disorders (4th Edition), Text Revision. Washington, DC: American Psychiatric Association, 2000.

19. Hamilton M. A rating scale for depression. *Journal of Neurology, Neurosurgery and Psychiatry* 1960;23:56-62.

20. Hamilton M. The assessment of anxiety states by rating. *British Journal Medical Psychology* 1959;32:50-55.

21. Scheier MF, Carver CS. Optimism, coping, and health: assessment and implications of generalized outcome expectancies. *Health Psychology* 1985;4(3): 219-247.

22. Underwood LG, Teresi JA. The daily spiritual experiences scale: Development, theoretical description, reliability, exploratory factor analysis, and preliminary construct validity using health-related data. *Annals of Behavioral Medicine* 2002; 24:22-33.

23. John D, Catherine T. MacArthur Research Network on Socioeconomic Status and Health. Salivary cortisol measurement, June 2000. Available from www.macses.ucsf. edu/Research/Allostatic/noebook/salivarycort.html. Accessed October 2, 2008.

24. Smyth J, Ockenfels MC, Porter L, et al. Stressors and mood measured on a momentary basis are associated with salivary cortisol secretion. *Psychoneuroendocrinology* 1998;23(4):353-370.

25. Teasdale JD, Zindel ZV, Soulsby, JM, et al. Prevention of relapse/recurrence in major depression by mindfulness-based cognitive therapy. *Journal of Consulting and Clinical Psychology* 2000;68(4):615-623.

26. Kandel ER. *In search of memory: The emergence of a new science of the mind.* New York: W. W. Norton Company, 2006, p. 342.

27. Schwartz JM, Stapp HP, Beauregard M. Quantum physics in neuroscience and psychology: A neurophysical model of mind-brain interaction. *Philosophical Transactions of The Royal Society London, B, Biological Sciences* 2005;360:1309-1327.

28. Rogan MT, Leon KS, Perez DL, Kandel ER. Distinct neuronal signatures for safety and danger in the amygdala and striatum of the mouse. *Neuron* 2005;46:309-320.

29. Kandel ER. *In search of memory: The emergence of a new science of the mind.* New York: W. W. Norton Company, 2006, p. 351.

30. Etkin A, Pittenger C, Polan HJ, Kandel ER. Toward a neurobiology of psychotherapy: Basic science and clinical applications. *Journal of Neuropsychiatry and Clinical Neuroscience* 2005;17:145-158.

Direct reprint requests to:

Peter A. Boelens, MD, MPH
1121 Grove Street
Vicksburg, MS 39180
e-mail: deltadoc@juno.com

APPENDIX D

Prayers Included in the Book

Scriptures Included in the Book

Recommended Healing Prayer Reading

1. *Healing* by Francis MacNutt, PhD
2. *Deliverance from Evil Spirits: A Practical Manual* by Francis MacNutt, PhD
3. *The Nearly Perfect Crime—How the Church Almost Killed the Ministry of Healing* by Francis MacNutt, PhD
4. *Let Jesus Heal Your Hidden Wounds—Cooperating with the Holy Spirit in Healing Ministry* by Brad Long and Cindy Strickler
5. *The Healing Touch* by Norma Dearing
6. *Healing Care, Healing Prayer* by Terry Wardle
7. *Inner Healing* by Mike Flynn and Doug Gregg
8. *The Mind and The Brain* by Jeffrey Schwartz, MD, and Sharon Begley
9. *The Spiritual Brain* by Mario Beauregard, PhD, and Denyse O'Leary
10. *Healing of Memories* by David A. Seamands

Order Form

Name _____

Address _____

City _____

State _____Zip _____

Daytime phone _____

Evening phone _____

E-mail address _____

Order

_____ copies of *Released to Soar* @ $13.00 each $_____

_____ copies of *Delta Doctor* @ $10.00 each $_____

_____ copies of *Where Next, Lord?* @ $10.00 each $_____

Shipping and Handling $_____

Shipping rate is $3.99 for one book, $4.98 for two books. For 3 books or more, shipping is free.

Total $_____

Please enclose check, cashier's check, or money order.

Send to:

The Write Place

599 228th Place

Pella, Iowa 50219

If you prefer, orders can also be placed online at:

www.thewriteplace.biz/bookplace